WHAT I'VE LEARNED SO FAR...

[handwritten note:]

Bee, I hope you enjoy this. It has been one of the most pleasant and rewarding projects I've ever taken on.

Fondly,

[signature]

April 28, 1993

WHAT I'VE LEARNED SO FAR...

BY THE STUDENTS AND STAFF
OF THE SPRINGFIELD, MISSOURI
PUBLIC SCHOOLS

Published by
THE SPRINGFIELD PUBLIC SCHOOLS FOUNDATION

**What I've Learned So Far... is that
if a school system has educational goals
for their students, provides the resources
necessary to achieve those goals,
holds students, teachers and administrators
accountable in a reasonable way,
and then gets out of the way and lets
the educators do their job...
educational miracles can happen.**

Ed Payton
President, Board of Education

Text and illustrations © 1993
by the Springfield Public Schools Foundation

All rights reserved
Published by the Springfield Public Schools Foundation
940 North Jefferson
Springfield, MO 65802

ISBN 0–9636553–0–1

Library of Congress Catalog Card Number: 93–84078
First edition, 1993
Printed by Litho Printers
Cassville, Missouri
Distributed by the Springfield Public Schools Foundation

PROLOGUE

The Springfield Public Schools Foundation was established as a conduit linking the community directly to its public school system. Through that linkage many good things are being made possible. Financial support from the Foundation allows teachers to bring to the classroom innovative new ideas that cannot be funded through the regular school budget. Given the opportunity, the Springfield community is stepping forward to demonstrate its belief that our schools deserve nothing less than the best that we can provide.

The book you are holding is an example of a Foundation project. The money for printing was provided by the Foundation. Sales from the book go into a permanent endowment earmarked for future writing projects and the interest earned will be available for teachers who need extra funds to create excitement and add special emphasis to the teaching of writing.

This project has been great fun. WHAT I'VE LEARNED SO FAR is one of those rare opportunities for an entire school system to focus on the same idea. Everyone took part. Kindergartners, nurses, high schoolers, teachers, administrators, bus drivers, principals, cooks, even the school board thought of lessons learned along the way. As you're about to discover, many of the following quotations are quite humorous. Others are straight from the heart. The range of thought and the topics of interest give eloquent testimony to the wonderful diversity in our public schools.

Some of the advice you'll read is practical: "Never go roller skating with a dress on." Some is philosophical: "Laughter is not always the best medicine, but it's a lot better than aspirin." Some wrestles with the great problems of life: "You never know what a girl is going to do." There are lessons in summarizing: "What I've learned so far is about worms, Columbus, and what to do in case of fire." On mother's love: "My mom has so many children she thinks she's rich." From vague feelings of distrust: "I don't like meatloaf because it has bumpy things in it." To tips for the beginning chef: "You can eat a chicken if you kill it." And many examples of early grappling with the politics of life: "What I've learned so far is to laugh at jokes, even though I don't get them...What I've learned is that little brothers don't listen unless you have a toy in your pocket...(and) What I've learned so far is don't play in your room if you have to clean it up, play in another room."

You're in for a treat. The 24,000 students and 2400 staff members of Springfield, Missouri's R–12 Public School System present WHAT I HAVE LEARNED SO FAR. There are many people to thank for making this project happen. First, the Foundation, for underwriting expenses of $10,000. Thanks go to Interim Superintendent, Conley Weiss; Assistant Superintendent for Secondary Education, Dr. Arnold (Bud) Greve; and Assistant Superintendent for Elementary Education, Dr. Ken Neale, for their enthusiastic endorsement and facilitation of the project. Thanks to their secretaries, Carol Roper, Judy Ferguson, and Norma Grantham for sending out reminders, answering questions, tracking down loose ends, and handling incoming submissions that numbered in the thousands.

Every principal in the system helped build enthusiasm for the book and from every building came at least one volunteer who worked hard to communicate to everyone in his or her school what the book was all about and to excite them enough to contribute their own wit and wisdom to the effort.

To the following teachers who acted as the editorial panel responsible for paring down more than 12,000 submissions to the 1,100 that appear in the finished product goes a special note of gratitude:

Jennifer Jackson (Twain)	Carolyn Malcolm (Williams)	Quinton Smith (Parkview)
Linda McFarland (Jeffries)	Marilee Howard (Fremont)	Sara Shelley (Cowden)
Kathy Hutchison (Sunshine)	Judy Brunner (Wilder)	Leslie Kilpatrick (Wilder)
Bob Shaw (Rountree)	Julia Fuller (Doling)	Carolyn Webb (Doling)
Anita Huff (York)	Niki Mott (Pleasant View)	Virginia Williamson (Retired)

Barbara Smith (Kickapoo) took the combined effort and tightened it into a finished manuscript. Dixie Neyer typed the manuscript so that it was camera ready for the printer. Linda Brewer (Study) and Carolyn Malcolm (Williams) proofread it all. Libby Hawkins (Pittman), Kathy Hutchison (Sunshine), and Cathy Warrick (Williams) obtained permission to publish all these authors and artists. Alishia Brundege, working with the elementary art staff, provided the book's delightful illustrations.

And what have I learned so far? Young people learn from the attitudes and actions of the adults around them—one way or another. If we fail to demonstrate directly to them how important we think their school activities are, that's another lesson learned. Their own attitudes as adults will reflect the manner in which the community treated them as children. What I've learned is that school systems and the quality of the education they can provide depend upon perceptions about the importance of learning that we build into our culture.

What I've also learned is that clear, logical writing leads to clear, logical thinking. Writing is a skill that must be learned. The love of words and writing must be inspired in each new generation and, in the absence of that love, the skill will never flourish. When elementary students have fun writing, the process becomes natural, ability improves, and young people develop one of the most vital tools we can give them—the freedom and the power of working with words.

Read the book. Send copies to friends and fan letters to the authors. It's a good way to demonstrate directly to them how important we think their school activities are.

David L. Harrison
May 1, 1993

WHAT I'VE LEARNED SO FAR IS . . .

To keep away from boys.
> *B. J. Roberts, Age 8, Pittman*

You can be rich and sad and poor and happy.
> *Allen, Age 10, Mann*

To accept what you are instead of what you wish to be.
> *Jessamyn Crosswhite, Age 11, Shady Dell*

You cannot hit someone hard enough to make them love you.
> *Quinton Smith, Teacher, Parkview*

Never color on the wall cause you get in trouble.
> *Randy Finney, Age 10, York*

That ditches stop cars very easily.
> *Damon Overboe, Age 16, Central*

That I can grow whenever I want to, the question is, do I want to?
> *Lethea Jones, Age 12, Weller*

It's not easy to do your homework when your book is at school.
> *Cameo McNeley, Age 9, Truman*

That in competition you can get your feelings hurt.
> *Lacey Randolph, Age 11, Pleasant View*

WHAT I'VE LEARNED SO FAR IS . . .

You can get everything you want and you'll want more.
Brandon Long, Age 12, Pittman

To not eat drugs.
Zach Hall, Age 7, Watkins

That prayer can never be banned from school; that is, as long as teachers give tests!
Spanky Price, Age 17, Hillcrest

That hair spray can't solve everything.
Colby Newman, Age 10, Horace Mann

Small deeds done are better than great deeds planned.
Charley Hawkins, Principal, Cherokee

That a girl at the age of 13 doesn't believe anything a male says.
Ben Winters, Age 13, Study

You can't put a boy and girl hamster together.
Michelle Walther, Age 9, Cherokee

That when you do something wrong, you have to face the punishment.
Michael Mathis, Age 11, Shady Dell

Some of the greatest times of your life are the shortest while the most painful last forever.
David Lane, Age 14, Phelps

WHAT I'VE LEARNED SO FAR IS . . .

The best love stories always start as friendships.
Shane Cockrell, Age 18, Kickapoo

How to paint a rainbow.
Janette Jilek, Age 6, York

My dog is a boy.
Tashia Renshaw, Age 11, Bissett

Our teacher knows everything, almost everything – I think.
Jackie Roberts, Age 8, Bingham

Escaping is worse than facing.
Taryn Lanza, Age 15, Kickapoo

That your mother knows most all of the things you do.
Robyn Taylor, Age 11, Gray

That on Friday we may get a Coca Cola award.
Nicholas Moses, Age 9, Shady Dell

You can't have everything you want, but sometimes if you ask politely, they might give it to you.
Josh Kindall, Age 12, Mark Twain

Don't put your homework on the floor, it will get thrown away.
Lee Hart, Age 10, Pittman

WHAT I'VE LEARNED SO FAR IS . . .

Eating too much doesn't solve anything.
Kristal Willis, Age 16, Central

Hamsters can get out of anything.
Chris Kabonic, Age 11, Cherokee

Nobody has a perfect life.
Roberta Herman, Age 8, Boyd

Life isn't easy when you get older and you have to have a college diploma to get most jobs.
Amie Hamrick, Age 12, Weller

That the taller I get, the more I bump into things.
Amber Hodge, Age 9, Cowden

Sitting on the couch watching TV commercials will get you nowhere in life.
Cathy White, Age 14, Study

Never to hit someone who has a big brother.
David Alford, Age 10, Shady Dell

Encouragement and praise are powerful motivators.
Sharon Montgomery, Teacher, Mark Twain

Paper airplanes and teachers don't mix.
Jeremy Blades, Age 13, Phelps

WHAT I'VE LEARNED SO FAR IS . . .

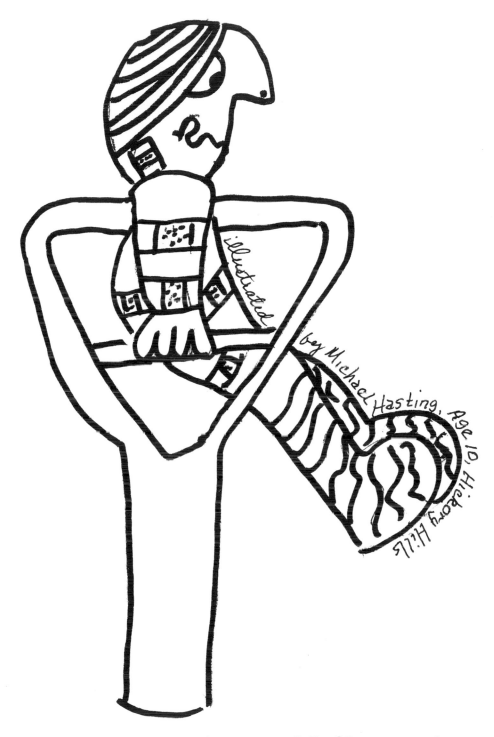

To never ride my bike in an alley full of loose gravel.
Mike Russell, Age 11, Robberson

WHAT I'VE LEARNED SO FAR IS . . .

How to be funny and not get in trouble for it in the classroom and get my work done on time.
Jose' Rojas, Age 11, Gray

That when you have a bad day, then you have a bad day.
Kevin Miller, Age 7, Sequiota

You can love as many boys as you want, but they won't always love you.
Hattie Farmer, Age 9, Weaver

A principal can predict a change in weather based on the "murmur" of children's voices in the lunchroom.
Sondra Pearcy, Principal, Portland

That I can do my hair, but my mom always comes and messes it up and does it again.
Sarah Hall, Age 8, Truman

The more chocolate you eat, the less appealing it becomes to you.
Danny Salyers, Age 13, Jarrett

When I sit around the house my mom makes me do a lot of work.
Kyle Jones, Age 10, Jeffries

Getting hurt isn't nearly as bad as hurting another.
John Wolfe, Age 17, Kickapoo

A little litter makes a lot of clutter.
Sarah Pope, Teacher, Mann

WHAT I'VE LEARNED SO FAR IS . . .

I am different from everybody else but I am proud of myself the way I am.

Jennifer Hales, Age 11, Weller

It is one thing to be old, but being old with fifteen cats is a different story.

Joe Barton, Age 15, Central

Mom was happy when I learned to ride my bike.

Britni Norton, Age 6, Mann

You don't have to do bad things to have friends.

Sarah Twitty, Age 11, Mark Twain

Perseverance is for more than a day.

Beverly Heinlein, Principal, Sunshine

Whenever you do something incredible like shooting at the basketball hoop backwards and making it, your friends are never watching.

Ramsey Mohsen, Age 10, Gray

If you have a friendship with someone, it is okay to fight.

Lindsay Scorpio, Age 10, Gray

Saying "I'm sorry" doesn't always fix what is broken.

Sally Hopkins, Age 14, Kickapoo

Never tell your teacher an excuse for not getting homework done, because my brother did that once and it didn't work out.

Brandi Tangora, Age 9, Mark Twain

WHAT I'VE LEARNED SO FAR IS . . .

The smarter you think you are, the more you need to learn.
Ben Roudenis, Age 11, Jeffries

Not to play with guns and not to smoke. Maybe I'll live longer.
Justin Watts, Age 7, Bingham

Some of life's disappointments are really some of life's blessings.
Heather Cole, Age 13, Jarrett

There's a little good in the worst of us, a little bad in the best of us, and we usually find what we're looking for.
Secretary AP Class, Kickapoo

Cowboys wore hankies to keep trail dust out of their mouths.
Josh Head, Age 8, Shady Dell

There is no dog big enough to eat all my homework.
Lara Santos, Age 17, Central

Recess is not the best part of school – the teacher is.
Jason Latimer, Age 10, Westport

When your cat insists on sleeping on your head, you will have a bad hair day.
Alishia Brundege, Art Specialist

You don't go to bed with gum in your mouth because in the morning it's in your hair.
Angela Telscher, Age 9, Delaware

WHAT I'VE LEARNED SO FAR IS . . .

Never argue with the tough guy that makes up the teams at recess.
> *Bryan Smith, Age 12, Sequiota*

When your mom says your first and middle and last name, you're in TROUBLE!
> *Lisa Myers, Age 9, Jeffries*

How to write the letter "I".
> *Stephanie Russell, Age 5, Twain*

No one likes to change a baby's pants.
> *Angela Kelley, Age 8, York*

You should never leave your guinea pig on your shoulder when you're playing Nintendo.
> *Kathleen Fergason, Age 10, Mann*

As a grandfather – the reassurance of my youngest grandson on losing his first tooth – "Don't worry, Grandpa, my tongue now has a window."
> *Bill Thomas, Member, Board of Education*

You shouldn't try to catch bumblebees.
> *Mendy Davis, Age 11, Pittman*

To always compliment mom about everything.
> *Aleah Weltha, Age 13, Reed*

"Knock your friends too much and pretty soon you will find that no one is at home."
> *Katy Bryan, Age 15, Kickapoo*

WHAT I'VE LEARNED SO FAR IS . . .

To not scream in stores.
Jennifer Hunt, Age 6, Cowden

WHAT I'VE LEARNED SO FAR IS . . .

You can never win against a younger family member.
Robert Beddoe, Age 11, Shady Dell

How to fold the laundry because it helps my mom and makes me feel good.
Tiffiny Harding, Age 6, Sherwood

The people who have their noses in the air never see where their feet are.
Jenni Jones, Age 16, Central

People are the only creatures who lie.
Lucas Johnson, Age 12, Pershing

I shouldn't always believe what is on T.V.
Danielle Love, Age 8, Rountree

You may have passion, consideration, and common interests, but love will surely die without communication.
Marianne Bell, Age 17, Kickapoo

Only the fool thinks he has all the answers.
Dennis Flattre, Teacher, Sunshine

Never stick your finger in a stapler!
Tony Netzer, Age 10, Twain

When you buy clothes, they always look better on you in the store.
Sarah Sneed, Age 12, Pershing

WHAT I'VE LEARNED SO FAR IS . . .

If you're trying to scare girls at a party, once you scare them, get out fast!

Justin Fravel, Age 10, Truman

It's a lot easier to stay up late than it is to wake up early.

Travis Heitheus, Age 13, Pershing

No matter what you do for your sister, they always like boys better.

Kristin Crawford, Age 11, Pittman

If you have some friends, it doesn't matter how small you are.

Kendra Schultz, Age 9, Cherokee

I want to be a scientist. I even know H + O = W.

Adam Protextor, Age 7, Sequiota

If mom's baking cookies, stay in the kitchen and you might get some.

Heather Nave, Age 10, Mann

Mothers do have eyes in the backs of their heads.

Misty Pratt, Age 14, Phelps

Books are better than movies.

Katherine Burgher, Age 9, Truman

It is fun but dangerous to climb down your laundry chute.

Beth Parsons, Age 11, Gray

WHAT I'VE LEARNED SO FAR IS . . .

Not to let my hair stick up in the air at picture time.
Melisa Arqueta, Age 11, Study

How to look back and see if there is a bee coming.
Jimmy Rich, Age 6, Pleasant View

School is hard after all, just like doing housework.
Amanda Hilton, Age 8, Twain

It's better to fall up the stairs than down.
Julia Dyson, Age 15, Kickapoo

If you try showing off with skates on, you fall down.
Brandon Larch, Age 11, Pittman

Never pour perfume in a fish bowl with fish in it.
Lauren LaPage, Age 9, Truman

There *is* a difference between hearing and listening.
Keri Barham, Age 12, Cherokee

Your heart is like a window – you need to open it up and let some light in.
Blythe Thompson, Age 13, Phelps

Never climb on the roof when it's snowing.
Colt Jeremiah, Age 10, Shady Dell

WHAT I'VE LEARNED SO FAR IS . . .

It isn't the number of scoops in a cone, it's the flavor of the ice cream.
> *Cara Coleman, Age 14, Kickapoo*

Not to write love letters.
> *Derek Wells, Age 7, Watkins*

No matter how old I am, I'm never famous.
> *Nate Kaunley, Age 9, Truman*

To get out, you have to find an opening.
> *Jay Jones, Age 17, Kickapoo*

Do not put rocks in snowballs.
> *Joseph Ferguson, Age 12, Williams*

You take yourself with you wherever you go.
> *Sondra Hagerman, Principal, Fremont*

You shouldn't try to make muffins if you don't have any milk.
> *Kelli Frankum, Age 10, Gray*

What I once thought was love was only extremely active hormones.
> *Joe Lister, Age 18, Kickapoo*

You're never too old to be afraid.
> *Misty Ashmore, Age 11, Bingham*

WHAT I'VE LEARNED SO FAR IS . . .

8x5 2x4 10x6 3x4 3x7 4x4 4x0 5x1 6x2 10x3 3x9 3x3 8x8

illustrated by Erin Gilbert, Age 9, Disney

If you leave laundry in a room by itself, it will multiply.
Toni Palmer, Teacher, Gray

WHAT I'VE LEARNED SO FAR IS . . .

✐ Some people are like blisters – they don't show up until the work is done.
> *Megan Mildenstein, Age 11, Bingham*

✂ My teacher puts a happy face on my band–aid and makes me happy.
> *Matthew Briggs, Age 6, Sherwood*

✐ Every freshman and sophomore in high school knows how many days until he/she receives a license to drive.
> *Brian Williamson, Age 15, Glendale*

✂ When you have a cold there isn't a REAL frog in your throat – I don't know why people say that.
> *Graham Chandler, Age 9, Delaware*

✐ Never to look at the labels on junk food if you ever want to enjoy eating it again.
> *Michelle Kaiser, Age 13, Phelps*

✂ In basketball, one person is not going to win the ball game, it takes a team to win a ball game.
> *Ryan Marquess, Age 10, Robberson*

✐ When my sister was chasing me and I looked behind me there was a metal pole in front of me and I hit my head on the pole.
> *Chad Cox, Age 8, Sequiota*

✂ In junior high, you have to fight your own battle in the halls.
> *Ashley Batson, Age 12, Jarrett*

✐ Don't eat caramels when you have a loose tooth.
> *Andrea Westhusing, Age 11, Pittman*

WHAT I'VE LEARNED SO FAR IS . . .

➤ That having a crush on someone can make you miserable.
   Jessica Barton, Age 11, Shady Dell

✄ Love doesn't cure all problems, but it is the ingredient of life that makes all things bearable.
   Mary Severn Hodge, Teacher, Watkins

➤ Laughter can be categorized as a "communicable disease."
   Yetunde Afulabi, Age 14, Kickapoo

✄ To look in my mom's closet for our Christmas presents.
   Tonia Carsten, Age 9, Bissett

➤ What is most important to me is most likely least important to 8 and 9 year olds.
   Jamie Nelson, Teacher, Wilder

✄ To laugh at jokes, even though I don't get them.
   Brooke Wise, Age 10, Jeffries

➤ If you take out the trash, you will stink.
   William Vernor, Age 8, Fairbanks

✄ Not to write notes in class.
   Jacquelyn Kindall, Age 13, Jarrett

➤ Green money is better than silver or copper change.
   Justin Roberts, Age 12, Westport

WHAT I'VE LEARNED SO FAR IS . . .

To sew up my Teddy bear.
David Sett, Age 7, York

By the time you accept and adopt a lifestyle, everything changes and no longer is your choice an option.
Donna J. Rodebush, Teacher, Pershing

Doing one handed cartwheels on ice can be really dangerous.
Kimberly McCann, Age 8, Truman

Every day should be a Friday – things don't seem to bother you as much on that day.
Debbie Burke, Teacher, Bingham

In math don't let the big numbers scare you.
Kryshia Scherff, Age 10, Sherwood

Nothing replaces a good sense of humor.
Joyce M. Creemer, Principal, Fairbanks

Family is the most important thing in life.
Ashley Birdsong, Age 10, Gray

Never let a compliment go unsaid.
Luisa Oyola, Age 17, Hillcrest

Never make a very long Christmas list because you don't get half of what you write down and your hand gets tired.
Kerri Hatcher, Age 11, Sherwood

WHAT I'VE LEARNED SO FAR IS . . .

Beautiful clothes, makeup and hair don't make a beautiful person.
Autumn Cook, Age 12, Jarrett

If he has a green Mohawk, don't bump into him.
Jeff Taylor, Age 16, Kickapoo

How to help my daddy wash the dishes.
Aimee Quick, Age 5, Gray

Not to fix a "bad hair day" with scissors.
Heidi Bleil, Age 15, Kickapoo

Yelling at my brother only makes my throat sore.
Lynn Knight, Age 9, Pleasant View

Below my bed is a perfect place to grow fungi for science projects.
Steve Linder, Age 13, Pershing

No matter how far away you are from friends and loved ones, they'll always be with you in your heart.
Rachel Gruber, Age 10, Twain

Too many people at this age are too self-conscious.
Jennifer Shadwick, Age 14, Central

You can't ride on a roller coaster if you are too short.
Brandon Lee Kirkland, Age 11, Bingham

WHAT I'VE LEARNED SO FAR IS . . .

Never walk and stare at the same time.
Holly Dunakin, Age 12, Campbell

WHAT I'VE LEARNED SO FAR IS . . .

Not to babysit for free.
Steve Jones, Age 10, Shady Dell

That a man cannot turn back into a boy.
Hongwei Chen, Age 6, Mann

Never ask your parents anything when they're paying the bills.
Joy Wasson, Age 12, Pershing

You really can look a teacher in the eye with an interested look on your face and still not have any idea what they are talking about.
Casey Vandeventer, Age 15, Glendale

That little kids get more attention.
Cody Duncan, Age 11, Pepperdine

To think about what you're doing and how you're going to do it.
Caleb Germeroth, Age 8, Gray

Discrimination doesn't exist in the minds of children.
Shannon Emerson, Age 13, Phelps

Sometimes you have to leave Springfield a few years, and return, to appreciate the warmth and resources of Springfield.
Sandra Harrison, Counselor, Kickapoo

Being a kid is the best.
Nikki Hudson, Age 9, Pittman

WHAT I'VE LEARNED SO FAR IS . . .

Kindness is the lubricant for the frictions of life.
Amy Johntson, Age 13, Pleasant View Middle

People are like books: some are much more than you expected and others require an extra amount of understanding.
Patti Provance, Teacher, York

No matter how good you are at basketball, the boys still don't pass you the ball to shoot.
Rebecca Cooper, Age 11, Phelps

Food is one of the best things for your body.
Emmanuel Ndem, Age 8, Truman

You only have 20 minutes to play.
Brandy Martin, Age 10, Study

Every child in this world is another hope for tomorrow.
Stephanie Slone, Age 12, Pershing

How I can read 460 books!
Britton Lutz, Age 7, Bingham

Sometimes just listening is better than any advice that could be given.
Becca Lewis, Age 14, Kickapoo

Each day is a true blessing from God and it is up to me to use it wisely.
Mae Tribble, Teacher, Weaver

WHAT I'VE LEARNED SO FAR IS . . .

To be kind to grownups.
Emily Miles, Age 6, Pleasant View

Knives are sharp, irons are hot, and women are smarter than men.
Shannon Emerson, Age 13, Phelps

How to read words like "the."
Brittany Childs, Age 5, Truman

The minute you allow one fifth grader to go to the bathroom, you have 26 more *needing* to go!
Jennifer Jackson, Teacher, Twain

How to eat real food like lobster and kiwi.
Lauren Peavey, Age 8, Rountree

I should have studied harder during my freshman year.
Chris Young, Age 17, Central

Who you really are is who you are inside.
Jennifer Damron, Age 9, Truman

Not to stand behind a cow.
Josh Williams, Age 11, Pittman

No matter how long you put alcohol on your face, you still get zits.
Neil Chambers, Age 12, Jarrett

WHAT I'VE LEARNED SO FAR IS . . .

The easiest way to drive my husband crazy is to hide the TV remote control.

Sara Johnson, Teacher, Robberson

To be nice to Derek as long as I'm at Bissett.

Misty Young, Age 10, Bissett

The best things in life are not things.

Nick Troxler, Age 14, Cherokee

No matter how hard you try, nothing will rhyme with "orange."

Annaliese Smith, Age 11, Pittman

Parents know more than you think.

Mindy McConnaughey, Age 11, Bingham

Everyone has cried one tear.

Alaina Wood, Age 9, Jeffries

How to have patience with the elderly and disabled.

Jessica Wilson, Age 10, Shady Dell

Girls can be very pretty inside no matter how they are on the outside.

Eric Whits, Age 13, Jarrett

If you live for tomorrow's happiness, you'll never be happy today.

Doug Jacobs, Age 16, Kickapoo

WHAT I'VE LEARNED SO FAR IS . . .

How to turn a cartwheel and make my hair touch the ground.
Meagan McCullough, Age 5, Sherwood

WHAT I'VE LEARNED SO FAR IS . . .

Laughter is not *always* the best medicine, but it's a lot better than aspirin.
Age 12, Pleasant View Middle

If you lose a friend, it's hard to get another.
Darren Lesch, Age 8, Pittman

It hurts when someone dies.
Suzanne Rodgers, Age 10, Cherokee

Not to lie because even if you don't get caught, it's not worth all the worrying you go through.
Heidi Bleil, Age 15, Kickapoo

Don't make your suitcase full if you know you can't carry it.
Kyle Loudis, Age 9, Disney

Life is a roller coaster so buy your tickets now.
Anthony Farris, Age 11, Bingham

You must learn to put your head in the water if you are going to swim.
Andrea Shapiro, Age 10, York

To always tell my mom and dad I didn't learn anything, but I really know everything.
Dustin Goodman, Age 6, Fremont

In bowling, if it hits the strike pocket, it won't be a strike.
Matt Rogers, Age 11, Pittman

WHAT I'VE LEARNED SO FAR IS . . .

When you throw something at somebody it is funny until you realize that they are actually hurt.
Richard Stewart, Age 16, Central

You can't walk big dogs – they walk you.
Jessica Kracman, Age 12, Jeffries

December is about Jesus and God.
Jeremy Burns, Age 6, Doling

That I don't know much.
Alicia Megee, Age 9, Wilder

Although you are a sixth grader, you have to take care of the little dudes if they need help, to set a good example for them.
Sam Hoover, Age 11, Bingham

No matter how much experience you have, nothing can replace pure luck.
Tracy Taylor, Age 13, Pershing

Not to swing after eating.
Brandi Adams, Age 10, Study

My kindergarten students believe I have the best job because I get to play all day. (I'm a P.E. teacher.)
Dianna Duncan, Teacher, Wilder

Never blow a big bubble in the hallways at school.
Adam Babcock, Age 14, Jarrett

WHAT I'VE LEARNED SO FAR IS . . .

You can't fold a piece of notebook paper more than 24 times.
Lonita Jamison, Age 10, Pittman

How to keep good care of me and my dad and mom.
Brandon Mires, Age 6, Cherokee

If there's something green on your plate, don't eat it.
Amanda Moses, Age 13, Study

I am thankful for what I have because some people don't have very much.
April Williams, Age 11, Watkins

You can't dress cats or they will bite.
Jessica Carden, Age 8, Truman

A blow to the face can heal, but a blow to the heart will scar.
Michael Field, Age 15, Kickapoo

When women become grandmothers they cut their hair.
Anna Barbel, Age 11, Phelps

Earthquakes can be fatal if not taken with caution.
Andy Cooper, Age 10, Pleasant View

You have to be taller than me to have a top locker.
Nichole Kimmons, Age 12, Reed

WHAT I'VE LEARNED SO FAR IS . . .

My numbers up to 8.
> *Misti Wilson, Age 5, Twain*

I make a difference in kids' lives.
> *Gloria Creed, Principal, Reed*

You should keep your temperature down, or you will be in a world of hurt.
> *Karl Palmer, Age 12, Weaver*

"Do you want fries with that?"
> *Kelly Robertson, Age 16, Kickapoo*

When my teacher says to do your work, she means it!
> *Carolyn Eastman, Age 7, Pittman*

Experimenting with your curiosity is the only way you can truly be original.
> *Angela Walker, Age 12, Phelps*

That Y = MX+B doesn't mean too much outside the classroom.
> *Jeremy Norris, Age 14, Kickapoo*

School cafeteria tator tots can be used for war.
> *Malachi Stowe, Age 9, Study*

How not to be mean when people are mean.
> *Brian Stephen Scott, Age 11, Truman*

WHAT I'VE LEARNED SO FAR IS . . .

You should never leave your guinea pig on your shoulder when you're playing *Nintendo*.

Kathleen Fergason, Age 10, Mann

A lawnmower that works earns money.
Josh Roberts, Age 12, Pershing

WHAT I'VE LEARNED SO FAR IS . . .

That you can paint with your feet!
>> *Jessie Rose Tyndal, Age 4, McDaniel*
>> *Early Childhood Program*

When you work at school on the weekends, you hear the ghosts.
>> *Mary June Hasty, Principal, Cowden*

Being made fun of hurts.
>> *Samantha Eveland, Age 9, Mann*

All nonconformists dress alike.
>> *Shannon Nichols, Age 16, Central*

No matter how innocent you look, your parents know you're guilty.
>> *Mike Reustle, Age 13, Jarrett*

It's a miracle when there are still paper towels in the bathroom.
>> *Jacob Harkins, Age 6, Pleasant View*

Never slow dance with a guy when someone, especially your mom, has a video camera.
>> *Rcena Denney, Age 13, Jarrett*

To always treat everybody equally and to never make fun of people who are different.
>> *Nathan Shelton, Age 10, Rountree*

Boys act goofy to impress.
>> *Stacy Westerman, Age 8, Study*

WHAT I'VE LEARNED SO FAR IS . . .

Deviled eggs aren't really eggs growing horns.
Jimmy Dinkins, Age 12, Jeffries

Not to feed a dog before a car trip.
Brent Slone, Age 10, Phelps

You can't have everything but you can try.
Adam Hoots, Age 8, Rountree

No matter how hard they try, your parents cannot be hip.
Harvey Westfall, Age 13, Pipkin

The words "Sticks and stones may break my bones but words can't hurt me" are not true.
Dustie Perrin, Age 9, Bissett

If you're clumsy, warn people you're going to be around.
Delayna Paxton, Age14, Reed

When I lick my cat, she won't lick me back.
Tory Steele, Age 7, Truman

An eye for an eye won't solve any problems.
Brandee Welch, Age 15, Kickapoo

You can't let a guy get in the way of your best friend.
Julie Thompson, Age 11, Cherokee

WHAT I'VE LEARNED SO FAR IS . . .

Never suck your thumb when you have a hang nail.
Jana Craig, Age 10, Twain

A true friend is like a rare book of which only one copy is made.
Mrs. Huba Ray, Counselor, Cherokee

Teachers care.
Matthew Wood, Age 8, Pleasant View

If you turn up your stereo loud enough, you can't hear your mom.
Matt Johnson, Age 11, Disney

Think before you glue.
Kennon Choate, Age 7, Fremont

Even a blind squirrel finds a nut.
Ella Stratton, Aide, Shady Dell

Eating junk food never helps anything, but, oh well.
Jill Turner, Age 12, Jarrett

It often takes great wisdom to know the difference between what is good for me and what is bad for me.
Judy Irwin, Counselor, Sunshine

If you don't have fun here, you won't have fun there.
Charlette Peterman, Age 11, Campbell

WHAT I'VE LEARNED SO FAR IS . . .

You never bother a snake or you might even get wrapped up by a python and you can't breathe and it kills you and eats you for dinner and it will hurt and you will be poisoned and you will have to go to the doctor.
Ronnie Higgins, Age 7, Weaver

The older you get, the more immature you used to be.
Julie Graden, Age 14, Kickapoo

The things you dislike in your parents' personalities are the things you inherit from them.
Jennifer Wolken, Age 13, Reed

Don't tell your sister anything unless you've got something on her.
Amanda Burros, Age 13, Study

How to hug.
Brandon Jones, Age 7, Bingham

Sometimes learning can be painful.
Stacy Whisler, Age 11, Mann

Sleeping with your hair in a pony tail doesn't make it easy to comb the next morning.
Jesica Stovall, Age 9, Pleasant View

In Biology IH, you should sit by someone smart.
Kim Elton, Age 14, Kickapoo

If you put a cookie jar in a room with a kid, there will be no more cookies.
Leah Macioce, Age 10, Jeffries

WHAT I'VE LEARNED SO FAR IS . . .

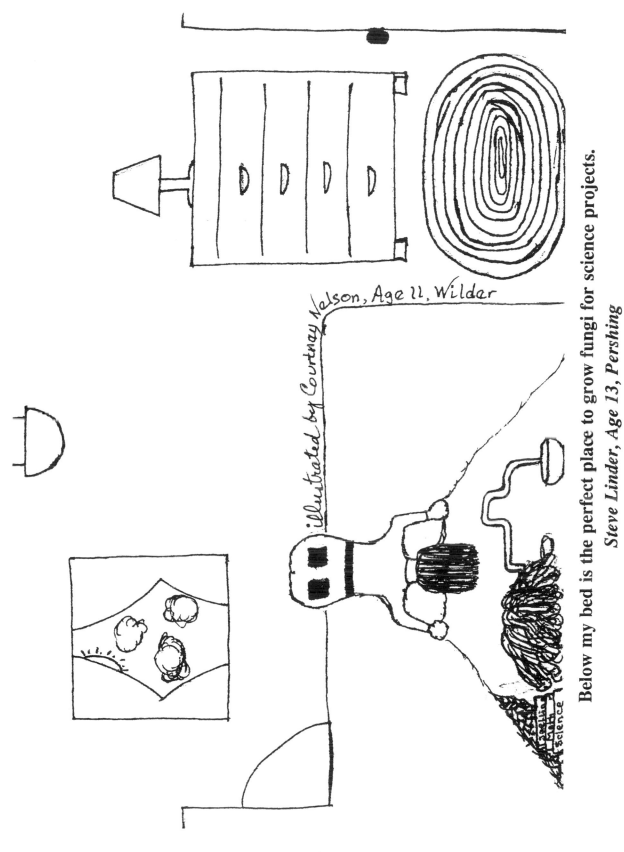

illustrated by Courtnay Nelson, Age 11, Wilder

Below my bed is the perfect place to grow fungi for science projects.
Steve Linder, Age 13, Pershing

WHAT I'VE LEARNED SO FAR IS . . .

Girls have feelings too.
Billy Sartin, Age 13, Study

Boys don't understand girl stuff.
Rachel Frank, Age 9, Portland

Rabbits like to run as much as people.
Ryan Hubbs, Age 6, Gray

The road to success isn't always straight.
Rena Morgan, Age 11, Mann

Not to change my hair style without getting permission from first grade students.
Ferba Lofton, Principal, Rountree

Boys are worse than I thought they were.
Jamie Smith, Age 8, Pittman

Animals can have many different purposes on earth and people too.
Brandon Ball, Age 10, Sunshine

Any person can accomplish any goal if he approaches the task with PEP! That's Preparation, Energy, and Persistence.
Dave Millsap, Assistant Principal
Pleasant View Middle

That my dad is my best friend in the whole world.
Cecil Kirk, Age 12, Westport

WHAT I'VE LEARNED SO FAR IS . . .

✏ You can trust yourself only if you really know yourself.
Jennifer Williams, Age 17, Parkview

✂ Joining in on things is more fun than sitting out.
Samantha Arnott, Age 10, Rountree

✏ If you're scared of the dark, it doesn't help to close your eyes.
Ryan Riggs, Age 16, Central

✂ There's nothing worse than a pencil without an eraser.
Rylan Rydberg, Teacher, Westport

✏ I need to go Christmas shopping earlier.
Melissa Crow, Age 10, Gray

✂ Sometimes you have to take charge of your fears.
Lacy Evans, Age 15, Kickapoo

✏ Life is like a locked door – you're stuck until you find the key.
Andy Summers, Age 13, Pleasant View Middle

✂ You can't make nothing from something.
Evan Austin Fisk, Age 9, Mann

✏ Women have more common sense than men, because man's best friend is a a dog – women's best friend is a diamond.
Jeni Parnell, Age 13, Jarrett

WHAT I'VE LEARNED SO FAR IS . . .

Once I loved a fifth grader and kept it a secret – I am still doing it.
Adam Presley, Age 7, Sequiota

If you go to bed with your hair wet, you will look like Albert Einstein the next morning.
David Morrison, Age 12, Study

My first and last name.
Stephanie Campbell, Age 5, Twain

When you're at the fair, don't eat before you go on a ride.
Kristy Gelsheimer, Age 11, Gray

Reality is for those who lack imagination.
James Brown, Age 18, Central

There's an inverse relationship between what I like and what's good for me.
Alex Hertzog, Age 13, Pershing

When you skin a snake you will find the meat.
Austin Shelnutt, Age 7, Truman

Parents cry too.
Jennifer Eiffert, Age 13, Cherokee

Self–discipline is the secret to a successful life.
David Tough, Age 16, Kickapoo

WHAT I'VE LEARNED SO FAR IS . . .

Boys only tease you when they like you.
Lindsey Cunio, Age 9, Mann

There's too much to learn.
Rachel Jones, Age 14, Glendale

The water isn't hot until you stick your finger under it.
Laura Ragan, Age 13, Cherokee

Not as much as my favorite teacher wants me to!
Freddie Thomas, Age 11, Weller

Santa Claus doesn't eat the cookies that I always leave out for him, my dad does.
Kedit Simphaly, Age 17, Central

Fathers are very sweet and nice even though they may get mad at times.
Whitney Moore, Age 8, Study

Never cover your mom's eyes when she's driving.
Sami Jordan, Age 11, Twain

When a tree grows, flowers grow and they fall off and apples go in their place.
Daniel Barker, Age 6, Gray

Never get in trouble before you ask your parents if you can go to a party.
Rebekah Grogan, Age 10, Pershing

WHAT I'VE LEARNED SO FAR IS . . .

Never color on the wall cause you get in trouble.
Randy Finney, Age 10, York

WHAT I'VE LEARNED SO FAR IS . . .

Dogs know how to sit, shake, and fetch,
but other than that, they don't know much.
Kelly Maloney, Age 10, Disney

WHAT I'VE LEARNED SO FAR IS . . .

High school girls like wearing a lot of weird stuff.
Bert Kelling, Age 10, Sequiota

The best you can do is all you can do.
Angela Trantham, Age 14, Kickapoo

Try to learn from your mistakes.
Brandon Brooke, Age 8, Bingham

No matter how bad your art work is, your mom will put it on the refrigerator.
Coe Parker, Age 13, Cherokee

It's hard to think while standing on your head.
Teresa Biagioni, Age 6, Mann

Responsibility is the key to success.
Jason Pool, Age 17, Kickapoo

I have learned that Mom and Dad don't always know what you think they know.
T. J. Spackman, Age 12, Phelps

Not to skate in the middle of the skating rink when you are little.
Matt Penprase, Age 9, Rountree

Always use a potholder to take cookies out of the oven.
Julie Johnson, Age 11, Bowerman

WHAT I'VE LEARNED SO FAR IS . . .

Never volunteer to do the fundraiser.
Lisa Peterson, Lunchroom Aide, Pittman

When you sharpen a pencil too much, you never get any work done.
Megan Bloom, Age 9, Gray

Never go into a decent place if you can't control yourself.
Machon Compton, Age 9, Twain

A child's hug is even better than an apple.
Marilyn Beach, Teacher, Wilder

It's been hard to live with all the changes in the world.
Steven Brezik, Age 11, Bowerman

That the Ninja at Six Flags will make you throw up.
Aaron O'Neal, Age 7, Sequiota

We need to be a little kinder to each other, to help each other a little more.
Tom Moorefield
Administrative Assistant to Superintendent

You have to be fair to others if you want them to be fair to you.
Tara Lawless, Age 8, Bingham

Life is stressful enough without running out of toothpaste and toilet paper.
Joyce Pyle, Teacher, Truman

WHAT I'VE LEARNED SO FAR IS . . .

Pain is temporary, pride is forever.
Jay Rogers, Age 14, Central

Life's not as easy as you think it is when you're young.
Jacob T. Scheve, Age 11, Sunshine

How to blow a bubble and how to do a back flip off the diving board and how to jump off the top of my tree house.
Megan Gregory, Age 8, Bingham

It takes a lot of air to play the flute.
Andrea Pachl, Age 11, Gray

You don't have to be the best at everything.
Nicole Brown, Age 13, Study

You should never get a triple decker ice cream cone.
Michelle Daily, Age 10, Twain

How important my heart is – I might not have to have a surgery again.
Lynsey McMillan, Age 6, Jeffries

Tie your shoes when you ride your bike.
Jenny Miller, Age 10, Pershing

Work is harder as you get older.
Tonia Lee, Age 9, Boyd

WHAT I'VE LEARNED SO FAR IS . . .

How to whistle!
> *Amanda Roylance, Age 5, Westport*
> *Early Childhood Program*

Turn your library books in on time or your pockets will be empty.
> *Barry Loudis, Age 12, Disney*

Having fun is an important part of life, when you're old and when you're young.
> *Jill Jackson, Age 15, Kickapoo*

Red ketchup is not blood.
> *Jared Templeton, Age 10, Truman*

If you don't speak out, people don't hear you.
> *Talli Ledwell, Age 13, Jarrett*

Staying up all night on a school night isn't fun the next day.
> *Ginger Dorrell, Age 11, Gray*

That I want kids.
> *Timothy Craven, Age 7, Bissett*

Not to go get a ball out of your neighbor's back yard if there's a big "Beware of Dog" sign on their gate.
> *Machon Compton, Age 9, Twain*

My favorite teachers come from my most difficult classes.
> *Suzi Shealy, Age 16, Central*

WHAT I'VE LEARNED SO FAR IS . . .

If you mess with girls, they will kick you.
Bobby Spurgeon, Age 12, Campbell

WHAT I'VE LEARNED SO FAR IS . . .

That I should be careful about what I say, because others remember.
> *Maryann Wakefield, Principal, Pittman*

A lawnmower that works earns money.
> *Josh Roberts, Age 12, Pershing*

If we do what we should, we won't have time to do what we shouldn't.
> *Jennifer Hill, Age 7, Wilder*

Life goes on no matter what happens.
> *Jennifer Brashears, Age 14, Kickapoo*

Respect is the key to life.
> *Brandy Blankenship, Age 11, Gray*

To love God and have Him in my heart.
> *Christina Jones, Age 9, Boyd*

Everybody has an opinion – some people use them more than others.
> *Lori Murphy, Age 17, Kickapoo*

Not to waste my money.
> *Jeremy Wilson, Age 8, Bingham*

About worms, Columbus, and what to do in case of fire.
> *Rebecca Owen, Age 10, Twain*

WHAT I'VE LEARNED SO FAR IS . . .

If you can get just a little help from someone, then you can do a lot more.
Holly Van Hoose, Age 13, Study

Getting my dog a warm bed for the winter won't help a bit because she'll just sleep under the shed.
Melissa Roberts, Age 11, Cowden

If I hide my squash in my napkin and throw it away, my mom will make me eat some more.
Joey Knight, Age 8, Pleasant View

About loving my mommy.
Ryan Williams, Age 6, Boyd

Being an only child has very little disadvantages.
Rina Edge, Age 11, Disney

It's best to look at someone by their personality.
Samuel Cheng, Age 10, Gray

Not to wipe slobber on my dad's shirt.
Hannah Carter, Age 4, McDaniel
Early Childhood Program

If you try, the outcome will always be better than if you don't try at all.
Nicole Butler, Age 14, Glendale

I can't just like a friend because she is cool or funny. It's what's inside that counts.
Tesah Tureaud, Age 10, Twain

WHAT I'VE LEARNED SO FAR IS . . .

There's nothing more powerful than your mom's hand.
Trisha Summers, Age 10, Fairbanks

Don't wear hair spray around an open flame.
Hannah Greenwood, Age 13, Jarrett

When you have a crush, your crush may not have a crush on you.
Ellen Creed, Age 11, York

White shoes don't look good for too long.
Nathan Pope, Age 13, Pipkin

Do not play with onions.
Amanda Oldham, Age 8, Boyd

It doesn't matter if your teacher is nice, mean, pretty, or ugly – what matters is that you learn something.
Megan Brantley, Age 10, Twain

No matter what you do, God still loves you.
Briggett Roberts, Age 7, Bingham

If you want an A+, study hard.
Jacob Schreiner, Age 11, Pittman

When you get in trouble and run away, it doesn't help anything.
Bernadette Esquivel, Age 9, Mann

WHAT I'VE LEARNED SO FAR IS . . .

The best results are from believing in yourself.
Kristin Johnson, Age 17, Kickapoo

How to ask for something instead of taking it.
Chris Hager, Age 11, Gray

If your brother calls you a dork, it means that you're a never-ending radical dude.
Shelly Criger, Age 9, Truman

Don't play football on a rocky field.
Caleb Floyd, Age 12, Bingham

The teachers that make you work hard are the ones that make you learn.
Sean Pennington, Age 10, Bowerman

Not to wrap rubber bands around my finger.
Kelly Brake, Age 6, York

No matter how bad things get, if you believe hard enough, they'll get better.
Brenna Day, Age 16, Central

That a know–it–all has few friends.
Becky Weiss, Teacher, Reed

School is more important than sports.
Jason Grant, Age 9, Mann

WHAT I'VE LEARNED SO FAR IS . . .

You have to be taller than me to have a top locker.
Nichole Kimmons, Age 12, Reed

WHAT I'VE LEARNED SO FAR IS . . .

Little brothers don't listen unless you have a toy in your pocket.
David Brandt, Age 12, Jeffries

A broken heart will heal.
Jennifer Brashears, Age 14, Kickapoo

When I think I've come up with the greatest idea, I find out that someone else thought of it years ago.
Moriah Stanley, Age 11, Cherokee

Rooms are good to sleep in but they are hard to keep clean.
Jenna Wixon, Age 7, Truman

How to ride my bike, how to share, how not to sin, not to cry, how to love, how to sing, how to be nice, what to do when I have a boo–boo.
Laura Ann Zirtas, Age 7, Mann

The very first piece of toilet paper is glued to the roll, but I have learned to get the piece off without it ripping!
Justin Lozano, Age 11, Fremont

Boys can't handle a girl when she is strong.
Sarah Cotton, Age 8, Truman

Friends are temporary, but family is forever.
Jereme Azeez, Age 13, Pleasant View Middle

It's not how old you are, it's how many miles you've gone.
Brad Kiser, Age 13, Jarrett

WHAT I'VE LEARNED SO FAR IS . . .

Life is like photography; it means nothing until you develop it.
Blythe Thompson, Age 13, Phelps

To be anything you have to learn math and stay away from girls.
Daniel Routh, Age 7, Truman

Kids are like the weather – changing constantly – pleasant one day – stormy the next – but tolerable most of the time.
Carolyn Shockley, Teacher, Pittman

Save up money for things you want.
Kyle Ezell, Age 8, Gray

You can't just all of a sudden tie your shoe, you've got to practice.
Angela Stoney, Age 11, York

If you're with your love, then anything you do is more fun.
Melanie Mathis, Age 18, Kickapoo

You can go places without your friends, and have fun.
Megan Maples, Age 9, Mann

Life does begin at 40 – it begins to fall apart: bifocals, over–weight, aches, pains . . .
Connie Cline, Teacher, Shady Dell

It is not hard to kick three boys at once.
Jessica Morelock, Age 12, Campbell

WHAT I'VE LEARNED SO FAR IS . . .

I carry the world in which I must live.
Karissa Kary, Age 16, Central

Boys are just as smart as girls.
Brittany Hunt, Age 8, Gray

The longer you wear the same socks, the more fuzzy stuff you get between your toes.
Austin Pitner, Age 14, Pershing

Girls can do anything that boys can.
Mendi Clark, Age 12, Reed

No matter how much I try to be different, I'm still me.
Candice Anderson, Age 9, Mann

Never pull a feather from your bird's tail.
Tiffany Banks, Age 10, Twain

To be good at my house and to be nice to my mom.
Reby Chadwick, Age 6, Truman

Verbs are important to me, and I will never forget them.
Marcella Benson, Age 11, Watkins

All worthwhile goals require patience.
Kellie Foster, Age 15, Kickapoo

WHAT I'VE LEARNED SO FAR IS . . .

Daylight Savings time doesn't save one much.
Dan Cogell, Teacher, Reed

When frogs get excited they hop.
Jill Ralls, Age 7, Mann

When a parent tells you to do something, it doesn't pay to get a second opinion.
Jennifer Stine, Age 16, Kickapoo

Cats and dogs don't live forever.
Leoma Shipp, Age 10, Portland

To play safely or you'll end up on your fanny.
Evin Pace, Age 8, Sequiota

How to get out of school restrooms when I accidentally get locked in them.
Judy Crisp, Teacher, Jarrett

How to love stuff like a Teddy bear and hug on my mom and dad.
Rachel Damron, Age 5, Truman

You can say a lot without moving your lips.
James Brown, Age 18, Central

Never, ever believe the weather man.
Laura Lavoie, Age 11, Sequiota

WHAT I'VE LEARNED SO FAR IS . . .

illustrated by Natalie Hamilton, Age 12, Hickory Hills

That you can paint with your feet.
*Jessie Rose Tyndal, Age 4, McDaniel
Early Childhood Program*

WHAT I'VE LEARNED SO FAR IS . . .

You can get more money from grandparents than anyone else.
Cody Mathre, Age 10, Mann

Laughter is a tranquilizer, except it has no side effects.
Yetunde Afulabi, Age 14, Kickapoo

Your life will get shorter and your memories get l–o–n–g–e–r.
Ben Hughes, Age 11, Sequiota

To take my own bath.
Jerry Wilken, Age 6, Boyd

The louder the music is, the better you think you can sing.
Lora Hansen, Age 12, Phelps

A teacher doesn't have to be serious all the time, or else the kids fall asleep zzzzzz!
Audrey Peer, Age 8, Field

Failure isn't really failure if a lesson is learned.
Maggie Armstrong, Age 13, Jarrett

If you don't speak up, your choice is already made for you.
Kris Myers, Age 11, Pittman

If you stay up for Santa, you will always fall asleep.
Rebecca Sanders, Age 9, Truman

WHAT I'VE LEARNED SO FAR IS . . .

That I like money and that I don't have it.
Kara Trapp, Age 11, Pleasant View

You should always have your parents sign progress reports when they're half awake.
Phil Cooper, Age 15, Kickapoo

To respect my country, the United States of America.
Scott Rothrock, Age 9, Twain

Winning isn't everything, but it is fun.
Alina Hamm, Age 12, Mann

To not touch fire.
Rochelle Logan, Age 7, Doling

You have to listen to your teacher or you get a call home.
Matt Kelley, Age 10, York

If you go hunting with your dad, you can't play around.
Jesse Browning, Age 8, Pepperdine

The fatter you get, the shorter your pants become.
Judy Palmer, Speech Pathologist, Shady Dell

Never attend a parent conference with purple ditto marks on your face.
Debbie Berger, Teacher, Pittman

WHAT I'VE LEARNED SO FAR IS . . .

Following Christ is more important than anything else.
Susan Hardison, Age 16, Parkview

To share the swing.
Ryan Books, Age 6, Boyd

Biting others may mean they'll bite you back.
Matthew Baumgartner, Age 8, York

Something that is hard is easy once you get used to it.
Jamie Hafner, Age 9, Twain

If you live in the country and your parents say you're going to town, don't trust them – you're probably going to the dentist.
Josh Evans, Age 10, Portland

A bad attitude is a bad idea.
Jacob Rushing, Age 11, Sequiota

When you give children a bath, use your elbow to test the water before you put them in it.
Rebecca Blanchard, Age 12, Watkins

About dinosaurs and how they lived and they died.
Joseph Bogue, Age 4, McDaniel
Early Childhood Program

Never wear mascara to the movies.
Olivia Morris, Age 14, Phelps

WHAT I'VE LEARNED SO FAR IS . . .

If you are making a C in art, life goes on.
Wes Davis, Age 13, Reed

No matter where you go, as long as you have someone who cares about you, you'll be all right.
Alex McHale, Age 11, Weller

How to gallop.
Brandi Bretz, Age 8, Bissett

Having a girlfriend is not embarrassing.
Billy Pollpeter, Age 10, Bowerman

We all need to laugh, but sometimes we need to be sad, too.
Christi Gilbert, Age 15, Central

Girls seem pretty but only from a distance.
Mike Curtman, Age 11, Bissett

Usually if you rush through your work, you have to do it over.
Kris Hurt, Age 9, Shady Dell

Most of us have seen stop signs, but not all of us acknowledge them.
Erin Curtis, Age 16, Glendale

When you make a fool of yourself and act like nothing has happened, your face gets just as red.
Jennifer Remy, Age 17, Kickapoo

WHAT I'VE LEARNED SO FAR IS . . .

The people who have their noses in the air never see where their feet are.

Jenni Jones
Age 16, Central

illustrated by Matt Rookstool
Age 9, Pleasant View

WHAT I'VE LEARNED SO FAR IS . . .

✏️ I can do almost anything I want to if I believe I can.
Michael Kimball, Age 9, Twain

✂️ Indians ground corn to make bread.
Magan Sanders, Age 6, York

✏️ When you're awake you want to go to sleep, and when you're in bed you want to get up.
Daniel Sample, Age 11, Pittman

✂️ Life is too short to let someone else ruin it for you!
Lisa Reece, Teacher, Kickapoo

✏️ Even if you lose, you're still a winner because you tried.
Angie Bland, Age 10, Jeffries

✂️ Nobody can say my name right, no matter how hard they try.
Creighton Vokoun, Age 14, Pershing

✏️ If you have a good book, don't put it down.
Brandon Cox, Age 10, Truman

✂️ About chores . . . I hate them.
Jeannette Hodgson, Age 8, McGregor

✏️ When you break something, don't try to hide it in the back yard, garage, or bottom of the trash can – hide it in the neighbor's trash can.
Katrina Lightfoot, Age 11, Wilder

WHAT I'VE LEARNED SO FAR IS . . .

Never put fingernail polish on as lipstick.
Daniela Novotny, Age 10, Twain

You grow up the day you have your first real laugh – at yourself.
Lori Swanson, Age 17, Kickapoo

Some people could be born with body parts missing.
Shalitha Laddimore, Age 12, Weller

It's OK to have ten boyfriends if five are in one state and five are in another state so you won't be trapped.
Alison Kate Warren, Age 7, Mann

When you are over 39, one of your most sincere students will approach you saying, "Mrs. P – you remind me of my great, great, great, great aunt who is in a nursing home."
Kay Powers, Teacher, Cherokee

You shouldn't eat candy or other things at school unless you bring enough to share.
Tommy Smith, Robberson

It does not really help to yell at someone when you are really mad at yourself.
Jenny Aaseby, Age 13, Jarrett

That Korin M. can PINCH!!!!
Asia Smith, Age 8, Truman

Working with children may be tiring, stressful, challenging, and rewarding, but never boring.
Beula Neuhart, Principal, Bowerman

WHAT I'VE LEARNED SO FAR IS . . .

If you forget your homework, you may as well forget your recess.
> *Erica Fender, Age 10, Twain*

My hands help me to learn.
> *Katie Aton, Age 6, Gray*

I'm the only one who can make myself happy.
> *Trishna Estes, Age 14, Kickapoo*

How I can spend money.
> *Justin Sherron, Age 9, Shady Dell*

No matter what you do, your parents love you.
> *Damon Turley, Age 12, Wilder*

Not all diamonds are girls' best friends – how many girls do you know who would happily settle for a baseball diamond?
> *Christopher Hoeman, Age 8, Field*

To do something different and not stick to the same old thing.
> *Davida Blakey, Age 11, Weller*

To learn you first have to listen.
> *Kelly Dann, Age 13, Jarrett*

To never ride my bike in an alley full of loose gravel.
> *Mike Russell, Age 11, Robberson*

WHAT I'VE LEARNED SO FAR IS . . .

The world turns around in a big circle.
Greg Lee, Age 5, Wilder

Life is like a bag of jelly beans: There are all sorts of colors and flavors.
Charisse Reiff, Age 18, Parkview

People have feelings and they don't want to be made fun of.
Justin Palmer, Age 10, York

The older you get the harder it is to run a race with dignity.
Marilyn Kleine, Teacher, Pittman

To count to 112 – then I get tired!
Lindsey Courtney, Age 7, Twain

You can turn an F on your grade card into a B.
Erick Webster, Age 11, Pittman

Worry is a waste of energy and time.
Karla Moore, Teacher, Cowden

Teachers will work you the hardest for the easiest test.
Carrie Gleason, Age 15, Kickapoo

When I fell out of a tree house it was plain old dumb.
Josh Jones, Age 9, Truman

WHAT I'VE LEARNED SO FAR IS . . .

illustrated by Ann Montgomery, Age 11, Wilder

You must pick up trash because it makes the world cleaner, and I like clean.
Alicia Moore, Age 5, Sherwood

WHAT I'VE LEARNED SO FAR IS . . .

To be good and that's all I can remember.
> *Jonnie Reed, Age 6, Williams*

Pizza doesn't solve everything.
> *Nick Gicinto, Age 12, Fremont*

I would only go around in circles if there were no obstacles to stand in the way.
> *Amanda Uffmann, Age 13, Jarrett*

Never to eat my Grandpa's chili.
> *Shevelle Todd, Age 11, Pittman*

Never let your dog in when it's pouring.
> *Anonymous, Age 10, Boyd*

Cheaters sometimes win.
> *Ashley Pruett, Age 14, Kickapoo*

Going to school is more fun than cleaning your basement by yourself.
> *Katie Davis, Age 9, Sequiota*

When a rose closes its petals, there is always a bud to take its place.
> *Angel Corwin, Age 16, Central*

Don't stick a crayola in a VCR.
> *Curtis Montgomery, Age 8, Pepperdine*

WHAT I'VE LEARNED SO FAR IS . . .

> Compliments and thank you's mean a lot more to us (and others) than we think.
> *Sarah Truman, Aide, Kickapoo*

> Teachers say to be quiet, but they're not!
> *Avery Mack, Age 8, Delaware*

> Just when you start going out with Mr. Perfect you find out Mr. Super–Perfect likes you.
> *Kari Bratvold, Age 15, Kickapoo*

> Not to put a knife in the toaster to get the toast out.
> *Ginny Fielder, Age 11, Robberson*

> You cannot eat as much as you want.
> *Steven Farrar, Age 7, Portland*

> Organization is the key, yet disorganization is a lot less stressful.
> *Matt Bentley, Age 17, Central*

> Dumb people do drugs, not smart people.
> *Christina Holland, Age 9, Westport*

> All students want to be successful; we, the educators, hold the key to unlocking the door to the alternative strategies or learning styles that will help them do so.
> *Ann Barefield*
> *Director of Curriculum and Instruction*

> Even sixth grade boys are afraid of brown beetles.
> *Rachel Dapp, Age 9, Truman*

WHAT I'VE LEARNED SO FAR IS . . .

Never walk and stare at something at the same time.
Holly Dunakin, Age 12, Campbell

Life isn't a cakewalk.
Joey Ashcroft, Age 11, Field

When you lay something down, next thing you know, it's gone.
Codi Walker, Age 9, Jeffries

When you get my mom, my sister and me together, you get a lot of makeup, hair spray, and fuss.
Talor Lafferty, Age 11, Shady Dell

Making new friends doesn't mean that you have to give up your old ones.
Jenny Tate, Age 13, Jarrett

Never sneak up behind my mom or I'm dead meat.
Daniela Novotny, Age 10, Twain

My whole name.
Frankie Norton, Age 6, Gray

There's no such thing as a boogie man.
Josh Watkins, Age 11, Bissett

Life can cause death.
James Brown, Age 18, Central

WHAT I'VE LEARNED SO FAR IS . . .

My teacher is kind and loves us all.
Joshua Hedger, Age 12, Twain

The only reason why teachers are teachers is that they love to be the one with the answers.
Melanie Pickering, Age 10, Phelps

Love could have a thousand meanings, but it means nothing until it is spoken.
Chris Huddleston, Age 16, Central

You should hide your underwear at camp or they will hang it on a flag pole.
Amanda Fay, Age 11, Shady Dell

If you can't trust yourself, you won't be able to trust anyone else.
Kim Butrick, Age 18, Kickapoo

What I didn't used to know.
David Reay, Age 7, Bingham

You can't have a boyfriend and a best friend at the same time.
Kari Lewis, Age 13, Pipkin

Most words in the world are hard to spell.
Ashley Hennigh, Age 9, York

When things are going good around school, ENJOY IT!
Dave Reynolds, Head Custodian, Hillcrest

WHAT I'VE LEARNED SO FAR IS . . .

illustrated by Amy Coleman, Age 10, Hickory Hills

Think before you glue.
Kennon Choate, Age 7, Fremont

WHAT I'VE LEARNED SO FAR IS . . .

Seek the truth, using reason rather than passion as your guide.
> *Nathan Nave, Age 18, Parkview*

Math is good to learn and if you're going to build houses, you'll need to know math.
> *David Huskisson, Age 9, Bowerman*

Life doesn't always have to be serious.
> *Cody Knight, Age 8, Pepperdine*

You must earn someone's trust.
> *Justin Butler, Age 13, Pleasant View Middle*

It doesn't matter how many goals you achieve; it matters what you used to achieve those goals!
> *Anonymous, Age 13, Pleasant View Middle*

At the most important times, I make the stupidest mistakes.
> *Nikki Howland, Age 11, Shady Dell*

Don't let strangers steal you.
> *Ashley Fleming, Age 6, Watkins*

All dreams take time and dedication.
> *Eryn Johnston, Age 14, Kickapoo*

You can't use it if you can't find it.
> *Noah Warren, Age 10, Jeffries*

WHAT I'VE LEARNED SO FAR IS . . .

➥ Not to ride a bike with your eyes closed.
    Jared Hutchinson, Age 11, Shady Dell

✂ Not to swing on the towel holder.
    Dedra Gann, Age 8, Bowerman

➥ Four–year–olds are not what you think they are because they'll turn around and hit you.
    Rheagan Stanley, Age 9, Jeffries

✂ You really don't know what you've learned until you have to put it into practice.
    Sarah Freeman, Aide, Kickapoo

➥ You can't solve anything by doing nothing.
    P. J. Deckard, Age 12, Twain

✂ If knowledge is power, and ignorance is bliss, life is compromise.
    Nathan Willis, Age 17, Kickapoo

➥ If you eat a lot of pie, it better not be pumpkin or apple.
    Geoffrey Zahn, Age 9, Twain

✂ How to wrestle snakes with three fingers around their heads.
    Steven Rothermel, Age 7, Fremont

➥ It is important to respect your elders.
    Melinda Pentecost, Age 11, Watkins

WHAT I'VE LEARNED SO FAR IS . . .

That horses are sweet and gentle.
Tiffany Crane, Age 11, Study

The smallest man with the biggest heart is greater than the biggest man with the smallest heart.
Ethan Hoerschgen, Age 14, Kickapoo

How to do back bends and splits.
Brandi Hoynacki, Age 11, Twain

That when I grow up I'll need a job, a house, and a car and gas.
Ryan Swearingin, Age 8, Campbell

To do something great, sometimes you have to be a leader and do it yourself.
Monica Giles, Age 13, Pleasant View Middle

Truly beautiful people like whoever you are.
Mike Freeman, Age 13, Phelps

If a dog licks you, it tickles.
Holly Magdziarz, Age 6, Truman

The hardest thing to do is usually the best thing to do.
Ben Dowdy, Age 10, Bingham

Don't play in your room if you have to clean it up – play in another room.
Lauren Edmonds, Age 9, Jeffries

WHAT I'VE LEARNED SO FAR IS . . .

That I can't do the monkey bars.
Katie Bench, Age 7, Pittman

God loves everyone in the world very much – He died on the cross for our sins.
Jamie Parks, Age 11, Watkins

You don't know what you're getting into until you have already gotten into it.
Chris Henderson, Age 12, Bingham

If you are going to become somebody, you have to achieve your goals and overcome the obstacles.
Becky Lumbert, Age 16, Central

Never go roller skating with a dress on.
Nicole Powell, Age 9, Twain

How to count my ABC's.
Scottie Keller, Age 5, York

I have not had "problem students" but I have had "students with problems."
Jim Boyd, Teacher, Kickapoo

Don't suck on the little hole on the side of a pen.
Jennifer Jones, Age 13, Jarrett

To be myself and not try to be someone I'm not.
Stephanie Shadwick, Age 10, Shady Dell

WHAT I'VE LEARNED SO FAR IS . . .

Illustrated by Kannon Lopaz, Age 10, Saquiota

A long time ago the Indians couldn't drive cars.
Christine Dittmer, Age 5, York

WHAT I'VE LEARNED SO FAR IS . . .

If you cheat people, they will cheat you back.
Jason Knadler, Age 11, Watkins

That 'right' has a lot of meanings.
Sean Butler, Age 14, Kickaqpoo

Not to be a snot.
Miranda Wilkins, Age 9, Bingham

No matter how much you think you know, you haven't learned enough.
Leslie Cox, Age 12, Bingham

Sixth graders are fun to be with – they know a lot more than people think.
Steve Banks, Teacher, Bowerman

To build tree houses.
Stephen Tyler Graves, Age 6, Williams

Teachers are sometimes old like 43.
Grant Ankrom, Age 9, Sequiota

Not to eat when half asleep.
D. J. Knakmuhs, Age 11, Shady Dell

Girls can be a pain!
Jon James, Age 10, Gray

WHAT I'VE LEARNED SO FAR IS . . .

When someone says to put your shoes and socks on – you don't really put your shoes on first.
Angela Cook, Age 8, Delaware

Life is like a roller coaster and, if at some point you find your car stops at a low place on the track, you may have to get out and push or play mechanic.
Rebecca Burt, Age 17, Parkview

Not to be told things twice, unless I want to be grounded.
Brandon Little, Age 11, Campbell

There is more to the heart than bump, bump, bump.
Chris William Balsters, Age 10, Truman

It hurts when your dog dies.
Matthew Malone, Age 9, Bowerman

Silence is sometimes the best way to express yourself.
Heather Wood, Age 15, Kickapoo

If you're nice to a person who is smaller than you are, you'll be their hero.
Tyler James, Age 12, Bingham

Everybody outgrows the peanut butter and jelly phase sometime.
Jennifer Boyd, Age 10, Pittman

If you give an alligator a cookie he will want to eat you too.
Ashley Nelson, Age 7, Cherokee

WHAT I'VE LEARNED SO FAR IS . . .

To be responsible and reliable so my friends can tell me secrets.
Sandi Mandrell, Age 12, Portland

A day with no laughter with others is a day wasted.
Helen Harber, Principal, Westport

Although the world is full of hate, there is a little spark of love in every heart.
Matt Bradley, Age 13, Phelps

To do circles.
Heather Johnson, 47 months, McDaniel Early Childhood Program

You should never give up hope in reaching your dreams and goals.
Jason Dingeldein, Age 16, Kickapoo

If you are mad or stressed, don't keep it inside – let your feelings out.
Amber Ghan, Age 10, Watkins

Always be honest no matter what the consequences are.
Kawana Washington, Age 14, Jarrett

Growing up is hard – you talk, you walk, and you go to school.
Georgia Watkins, Age 8, Campbell

There are more smart people than crazy people, but there's still a heck of a lot of crazy people.
Kyle DePew, Age 11, Jeffries

WHAT I'VE LEARNED SO FAR IS . . .

A good man is hard to find, but if you find one, hang on tight.
Beverly Farrand, Teacher, Shady Dell

An apple a day doesn't keep the doctor away—trust me, I've tried it.
Sarah Giboney, Age 15, Glendale

Even when I "thunk and thunk and thunk," I'm still not sure if I go to Prime Time or ride the bus home.
Cody Sherman, Age 6, Pleasant View

Late TV doesn't get me to school on time.
Christa Johnston, Age 6, Bingham

The anticipation of something is often better than having it.
Libby Hawkins, Teacher, Pittman

You have to be careful what you give away to friends.
Kellie Buchanan, Age 10, Gray

Only you can make things better.
Marcia Bisher, Food Service, Bowerman

Discovering you're good at something is the best discovery of all.
Valter Herman, Age 16, Central

At school, if you don't want *everyone* to know something, don't tell *anyone*.
J. D. Kosal, Age 11, Jeffries

WHAT I'VE LEARNED SO FAR IS . . .

The easiest way to drive my husband crazy is to hide the TV remote control.
Sara Johnson, Teacher, Robberson

WHAT I'VE LEARNED SO FAR IS . . .

In life, you don't get everything you want.
Jeremiah Hayes, Age 11, Watkins

About different parts of pumpkins, their seeds, and pie.
Joshua Mendenhall, Age 6, Williams

How to get along with people who don't always get along with me.
Kristina Nicol Lee, Age 10, Gray

Growing up takes a long time, but not for a cat.
Joshua Elkins, Age 8, Campbell

It's better to push yourself than to be pushed by others.
Thomas Lampe, Age 14, Jarrett

Not to laugh when I'm drinking water.
Justin Wilson, Age 9, Twain

You can get in trouble for things you didn't even know were bad.
Peter Langston, Age 12, Pershing

Words hit harder than fists.
Lauren Willard, Age 13, Phelps

With a sister it's hard to get to be alone.
Rose Allen Hoerner, Age 11, Portland

WHAT I'VE LEARNED SO FAR IS . . .

➤ How to tell you're getting older besides looking in the mirror – when I first started teaching kindergarten, sometimes they called me Mother . . . now they call me Grandma.
Pat Wright, Teacher, Doling

✁ Money is made from paper instead of tree leaves, so that parents can tell their children that money doesn't grow on trees.
Angie Bahr, Age 17, Parkview

➤ There is a lot more to learn in life than I already know, and I won't live long enough to learn nearly everything.
Patrick Johnson, Age 11, Weller

✁ Two times you need to keep your mouth shut are when you're swimming and when you're angry.
Kate Johnson, Age 13, Jarrett

➤ When Dad comes in the door, it's his turn to watch TV!
Layne Henslee, Age 9, Jeffries

✁ My boyfriend can love more than one girl.
Miranda Harris, Age 7, Pittman

➤ If you make a mistake, it is OK.
Delynne Baney, Age 10, Disney

✁ While usual may be just fine, different is much more interesting.
Michelle Miller, Age 12, Phelps

➤ To half–way tie my shoe.
Ryan Burrell, Age 8, Watkins

WHAT I'VE LEARNED SO FAR IS . . .

✏ Responsibility is a hard thing.
Ginney Norton, Age 10, Gray

✂ No matter how hard you pray, God won't clean your room for you.
Jill Weimer, Age 14, Kickapoo

✏ If you do stuff right the first time, you don't have to do it again.
Misty Alcorn, Age 11, Portland

✂ How to say NO in several different ways.
Lesa Collins, Teacher, Bowerman

✏ Never try to fix a broken TV.
Casey Greene, Age 9, Twain

✂ If you have an ant farm, you have to *feed* the ants.
Lucas Johnson, Age 12, Pershing

✏ Not to go behind cows, pigs, and horses.
Angela Hickman, Age 7, Sequiota

✂ Youth is like the ozone layer, once it's gone it's gone forever, so take care of it while you can.
Jennifer Jiz, Age 17, Kickapoo

✏ About the time you figure out all the answers to life, the questions change.
Lori Inman, Teacher, Pittman

WHAT I'VE LEARNED SO FAR IS . . .

When two or more people work together, a task becomes easier.
Katie Black, Age 10, Pleasant View

When I've had a bad day, I don't need advice, just a warm hug!
Kari Bratvold, Age 15, Kickapoo

A long time ago the Indians couldn't drive cars.
Christine Dittmer, Age 5, York

When you put a jacket on a monkey, it looks silly.
Jeremy Teppo, Age 13, Campbell

No one lives long enough to learn from their mistakes, so watch other people's along the way.
Eric Dwayne, Age 16, Central

I should try not to be afraid to read my story in front of the class.
Elizabeth Clouse, Age 7, Pittman

What you say isn't always what is heard.
Elaine Emry, Teacher, Twain

Mostly to tell right from wrong.
Galen Scroggins, Age 11, Bingham

Trust God during the difficult times, even though you may feel like blaming Him for them.
Julie Brueggemann, Age 17, Parkview

WHAT I'VE LEARNED SO FAR IS . . .

Illustrated by Adrienne Gilbert, Age 9, Disney

Not to put an ice cube in my brother's diaper.
Lauri Simmons, Age 7, York

WHAT I'VE LEARNED SO FAR IS . . .

There is no such thing as time, only appointments.
Cameron Mott, Age 14, Kickapoo

To give everyone a chance to be a friend.
Kassie Maner, Age 11, Williams

Friends don't always stay your friends, so you'd better enjoy them while you have them.
Lotus R. Spradlin, Age 11, Rountree

You have to learn how to be a loser before you can be a winner.
Canda Crawford, Age 9, Twain

If I want a lunch ticket, I need to bring money.
Kelly Durden, Age 6, Bingham

If you read a book, you feel like you're in the story.
Joey Jones, Age 10, Disney

Grownups get to do what they want and they get to have all the food they want.
Tiffany Gardner, Age 8, Campbell

Never mess with a teacher who talks to himself.
Wanjiku Njroge , Age 13, Jarrett

Wherever I go, girls are always trouble.
Ryan Painter, Age 10, Cowden

WHAT I'VE LEARNED SO FAR IS . . .

Do not put chocolate sauce in coffee.
Ashlee Jane Bellamy, Age 9, Truman

Not to stick my finger in a baby's open mouth.
Heather Terry, Age 11, Bingham

Love makes you feel warm inside.
Matthew Hammond, Age 8, Campbell

Friends come and friends go, but enemies accumulate.
Chad White, Age 18, Parkview

To play with the new kids because you can be their friend.
Evan Wolters, Age 7, Mann

Nothing goes "pop" on a pop quiz.
John Haines, Age 16, Central

If we learn from our mistakes, I ought to be a genius.
Rebecca Drury, Age 12, Pershing

Dogs know how to sit, shake, and fetch, but other than that, they don't know much.
Kelly Maloney, Age 10, Disney

Milk tastes just as good when you drink it out of the jug.
Laura Cummings, Prime Time Prevent, Pittman

WHAT I'VE LEARNED SO FAR IS . . .

Being someone else does not help you get friends.
Melina Auston, Age 8, Jeffries

If opportunity doesn't knock, you should build a door.
Cameron Mott, Age 14, Kickapoo

Books aren't as easy as I thought to write.
Amber Meadows, Age 11, Boyd

How to work with partners.
Jennifer Gaddy, Age 8, Portland

One pound of chocolate = 10 pounds of fat.
Janel Olsen, Age 12, Pershing

Your mom can agree with you sometimes.
Amber Shelnutt, Age 9, Truman

No matter how awake you are, you can always sleep through Algebra.
Kelly Luginsky, Age 13, Jarrett

I can talk, and make books, and do anything I try to do.
Marquita Watts, Age 6, Fremont

You never know what a girl is going to do.
Chris Nanninga, Age 11, Twain

WHAT I'VE LEARNED SO FAR IS . . .

I've learned that teaching school is hardest at Christmas time, in spring time, when there's a full moon, when the weather's turning bad, etc.
Patty Chambers, Teacher, Weaver

The stuff you have to remember, you forget, and the stuff you don't have to remember, you will never forget.
Alexis Webb, Age 13, Phelps

Treat people with respect, and the rest is too long to put on this piece of paper.
Laine Blackwell, Age 11, Rountree

The best part of a dance is talking about everyone's dress.
Kari Bratvold, Age 15, Kickapoo

Boys can get you into a lot of trouble.
Amanda DeLapp, Age 7, Gray

If you give respect to kids, they give it back.
Sally Nehring, Teacher, Mann

How to be a friend and make a friend.
Tasha Lynn Loomis, Age 8, Twain

Whenever "housework" is mentioned, my brother disappears.
Katie Rahmeyer, Age 13, Jarrett

Pigs in a blanket are not really real pigs in real blankets.
Ryan Yarham, Age 10, Jeffries

WHAT I'VE LEARNED SO FAR IS . . .

Not to put a knife in the toaster to get the toast out.
Ginny Fielder, Age 11, Robberson

Not to take off my suspenders because I can't get them back on again.
Dylan Spruance, Age 5, Sherwood

WHAT I'VE LEARNED SO FAR IS . . .

To keep my eyes open to the world, so that the world can open my eyes.
Erin Jones, Age 16, Glendale

No matter where you go, math will always be there.
Scott McLean, Age 11, Bingham

Even though we're all different, we should be treated the same.
Nick Byers, Age 8, Mann

If you lose, but keep trying and learning from your mistakes, you will become a winner in the end.
Christina Peterman, Age 12, Jarrett

How to open the milk carton on the right side, not the wrong side.
Landry Jones, Age 9, Gray

Don't smoke.
Blaine Boyle, Age 6, Watkins

When you finish the race a winner, the pain disappears.
Kari Donnell, Age 14, Kickapoo

No matter how small you are, how big you are inside is all that matters.
April Kincheloe, Age 10, Jeffries

It's easier to do homework after you check it in class, but you don't always get away with it.
Brad Palmer, Age 13, Jarrett

WHAT I'VE LEARNED SO FAR IS . . .

People are like flowers, some bloom after others.
Jenni Jones, Age 16, Central

You can't tell if people are nice or mean by how they look.
Jeremy See, Age 9, Gray

You can't bribe a teacher.
Cody Lee Castell, Age 13, Pershing

It's important to have feelings and show them instead of hiding them.
Kimberly Redd, Age 11, Bingham

When the fireplace burns up the house, I know it is time to get out.
Andy Brouwer, Age 8, Mann

Winning is related to one's expectations: expect first, get second – it's a downer. Expect sixth, get second – wow!
Judy Talley, Coach, Kickapoo

Books are my best friends and they always will be.
Sara Green, Age 10, Disney

Despite life's difficulties and hardships, it's important to keep my head held high and have faith that I can overcome anything.
Kim Holland, Age 17, Kickapoo

You can't touch a star.
Dustin Burns, Age 7, York

WHAT I'VE LEARNED SO FAR IS . . .

Saying "Goodbye" is never easy, no matter what.
Sarah McIntyre, Age 13, Pleasant View Middle

There are three kinds of people in the world – people who are good at math and people who are not.
Phill Harris, Age 12, Pershing

No matter how hard you try, you can't budget your allowance and buy all the CD's you want at the same time.
David Summers, Age 11, Wilder

Girls aren't everything, but pretty close to it.
Jared Stratton, Age 14, Kickapoo

If you do your best in things, your parents will be proud.
Jessica Talbot, Age 10, Gray

It is hard to cook when the stove blows up.
Andy Brouwer, Age 8, Mann

Everyone has strengths and weaknesses and you need to respect that.
Joshua Horn, Age 11, Bingham

You can't wiggle in church.
Laura Aderhold, Age 9, Rountree

It takes a lifetime to have a friend for life.
Alison Strunk, Age 12, Jarrett

WHAT I'VE LEARNED SO FAR IS . . .

Nothing tastes sweeter than success – except chocolate ice cream.
> *Carissa Stivers, Age 17, Kickapoo*

It doesn't matter how many years you go to school if you don't pay attention.
> *Becca Ansley, Age 10, Phelps*

I've learned how to count to 1,010.
> *Jason Lightner, Age 7, Twain*

Not everyone is born with a silver spoon, but one can do a lot with wood.
> *Marilyn Harris, Teacher, Pershing*

The more I learn, the more I understand.
> *Mike Caldwell, Age 13, Jarrett*

Friends fight over the silliest stuff.
> *Amanda Carr, Age 10, Campbell*

You've got to constantly look at yourself to make sure you never become what you hate.
> *Steve Duggar, Age 15, Central*

If you don't water a plant, it won't grow.
> *Jessica Harris, Age 9, Fairbanks*

When I play on the computer, I can't bang on the keys.
> *Brandon Plumb, Age 5, York*

WHAT I'VE LEARNED SO FAR IS . . .

It is hard to cook when the stove blows up.
Andy Brouwer, Age 8, Mann

WHAT I'VE LEARNED SO FAR IS . . .

Don't play basketball outside with the Christmas lights up.
Steve Lindley, Age 12, Jarrett

Never stand behind someone spraying a wasps' nest.
Nathan Gilbert, Age 11, Bingham

Not to put an ice cube in my brother's diaper.
Lauri Simmons, Age 7, York

If mom can't fix it, grandma will.
Julie Appleby, Age 14, Kickapoo

You don't get to keep your friends for all of your life.
Dior Spellman, Age 10, Pittman

You should always go with your first instinct.
Amy Liddle, Age 14, Pleasant View Middle

It's not easy being the youngest in the family.
Rebecca Bradley, Age 8, Mann

Make sure your sister has clipped her fingernails before you pinch her.
Megan Walker, Age 11, Disney

You take what you've got and deal with it.
Heidi Brown, Age 13, Jarrett

WHAT I'VE LEARNED SO FAR IS . . .

The very worst thing you can ever ever do is give up.
Lindsey Saunders, Age 11, Phelps

When your teacher tells you to sit, you sit.
Stacey Flippo, Age 9, Cowden

The best way to learn is to have fun because you learn and so does your teacher.
Renee Evans, Age 12, Robberson

It is smart to think when you are doing a test.
Andy Denney, Age 10, Gray

Freedom of thought is repressed voluntarily.
Mark Tweedy, Age 16, Kickapoo

Problems relating to my child are harder on me than on her.
Bonnee Griggs, Teacher, Mann

To tell the weather.
Stephanie Fawver, Age 6, Twain

If you keep on practicing something, you will get better at it.
Sheri Dayton, Age 11, Bingham

When pressures are on you, you can't think as well as usual.
Nick Byers, Age 8, Mann

WHAT I'VE LEARNED SO FAR IS . . .

No matter how early you wake up, you never get to the bathroom first.
Jessica Hatfield, Age 11, Phelps

Charlie Brown is still my greatest hero.
Joan Liu, Age 16, Kickapoo

Not to talk when others talk, because others can't hear.
Jessica Bueno, Age 7, Williams

When a watch says it is not waterproof, it is not lying.
Crystal Hamilton, Age 11, Gray

Kids love to be smiled at.
Sherri Devries, Teacher, Bowerman

No matter how many times you try to get rid of a little sister, she always comes back.
Christa Snider, Age 10, Twain

To be brave and learn to write in cursive and don't cry if you fall down, not unless you have to.
Laura Johnson, Age 9, Cowden

Clothes and hair aren't the most important things in the world.
Andrea Diamond, Age 14, Kickapoo

Don't think twice about something, because if you do you will never get anything done.
Emily Lawson, Age 10, Bingham

WHAT I'VE LEARNED SO FAR IS . . .

There are two things our parents are required to give us – one is roots, the other is wings.
Erik Janeczko, Age 15, Glendale

To never mess around with my lunchroom attendant.
Adam Fall, Age 12, Sequiota

You can't get blood from a turnip and you can't get homework from Scott.
Anonymous, Teacher, Boyd

You learn a lot each day.
Cheston Doran, Age 9, Gray

There are no monsters in the closet.
Brandii Hester, Age 10, Westport

Nothing in life is worth deceiving a friend for.
Mark Walker, Age 15, Kickapoo

If you buy a hamburger you are really buying a piece of cow.
Brian Jowett, Age 13, Pershing

The older I get, the better I like family traditions and rituals.
Mary Masters, Parent Educator
with Parents As Teachers

How to get along a little bit.
Lacey Dempsey, Age 9, Twain

WHAT I'VE LEARNED SO FAR IS . . .

It's one thing to be old, but being old with fifteen cats is another story.
Joe Barton, Age 16, Central

WHAT I'VE LEARNED SO FAR IS . . .

It's a good feeling to know you've done something well.
John Zeien, Age 11, Mann

The little voice inside me is usually right.
Jennifer Stine, Age 16, Kickapoo

You have more friends than you think.
Casey Miller, Age 9, Twain

I don't like meatloaf because it has bumpy things in it.
Dustin Rice, Age 6, Wilder

How to take responsibility to watch little babies ages 7 months to 6 years old.
Micheala Smith, Age 12, Twain

There are a lot of people who care.
Mechelle Tucker, Age 11, Portland

Not to be afraid to ask people stuff. Don't lie, either, because it's not right.
Sam Dorrough, Age 8, Delaware

The directions are the best advice on how to put something together.
Olivia Morris, Age 14, Phelps

You get friends, like them, and sometimes lose them.
Eric Sonnakolb, Age 10, Campbell

WHAT I'VE LEARNED SO FAR IS . . .

Not to eat other people's food.
Adam Ebright, Age 6, York

Never do something because your friends do it.
Kawana Washington, Age 14, Jarrett

When I see a preschool child in a wheelchair, I no longer see the chair.
Judy Brunner, Principal, Wilder

Getting locked out of the car when it's pouring down rain is not too good.
Jessica Isbell, Age 9, Fremont

You can't have it your way 'cause this is not Burger King.
Matt Happle, Age 12, Cherokee

The least expensive investment yielding the highest dividend is a thank you.
Ruth Martin, Teacher, York

It's not too smart to let your little brother or sister play in the dog's water.
Jessica Cook, Age 8, Bowerman

Never drink orange juice and milk together because you will throw up.
Melanie Bond, Age 11, Bingham

Long nights and all A+'s are related.
Katie Kring, Age 9, Disney

WHAT I'VE LEARNED SO FAR IS . . .

The inside of a pumpkin is icky.
Michelle Freeman, Age 6, Wilder

To turn the ceiling fan off before climbing up a bunk bed.
Joey Carney, Age 12, Pittman

After 33 years of teaching Driver's Ed, the following are "No Passing" zones: hills, curves, intersections, railroad crossings, and beyond the line of scrimmage.
Clifford McLain, Teacher, Parkview

Sometimes you need a little help.
Abby Pitts, Age 9, Delaware

Through life's struggles, God brings hope and faith, and He never lets you down.
Jenny McClaflin, Age 14, Pleasant View Middle

At times I'm the only person with a sense of humor.
Brian Carlstrom, Age 11, Twain

Not to give in to peer pressure.
Andy White, Age 14, Jarrett

I can read and write but I just can't understand my sister.
Valerie Gaines, Age 10, Disney

Don't worry about what people *think;* worry about what they know.
Janet Chambers, Age 17, Kickapoo

WHAT I'VE LEARNED SO FAR IS . . .

A smile in any language means happiness.
Ben Hughes, Age 11, Twain

Don't put dirt in your mouth because you can get sick.
Karissa Arnold, Age 9, Delaware

If you marry the wrong person, you know right away. If you marry the right one, you're never totally sure.
Anonymous, Cowden

The affections of a girl are not to be toyed with.
Kevin Holdt, Age 12, Shady Dell

It's not easy to get what you want.
David Ashlin, Age 10, Gray

What I say is not always what my students hear.
Sara Shelley, Teacher, Cowden

Not to take off my suspenders, because I can't get them back on again.
Dylan Spruance, Age 5, Sherwood

You can't make a complete sentence without a noun and you can't have a complete class without a clown.
Natasha Mandl, Age 13, Jarrett

To not stick my tongue out.
Miranda Rivet, Age 7, York

WHAT I'VE LEARNED SO FAR IS . . .

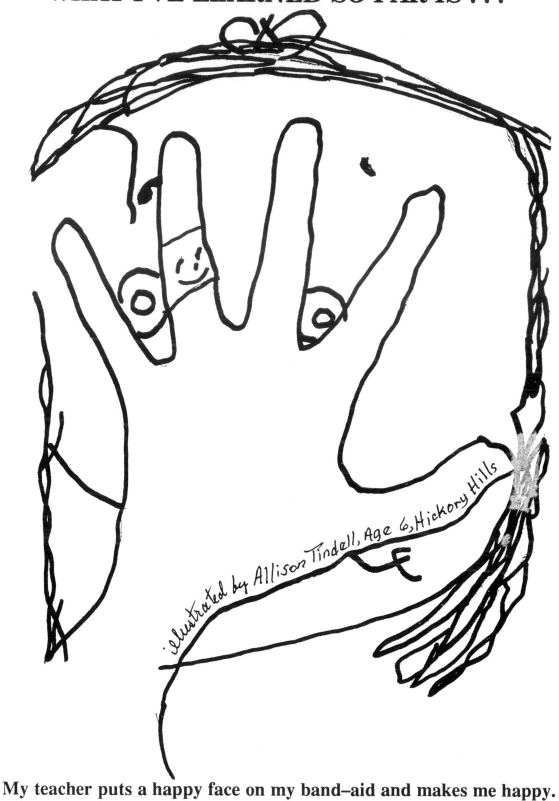

illustrated by Allison Tindell, Age 6, Hickory Hills

My teacher puts a happy face on my band–aid and makes me happy.
Matthew Briggs, Age 6, Sherwood

WHAT I'VE LEARNED SO FAR IS . . .

There is always someone's head in the way at an assembly.
Brian Wilson, Age 8, Bowerman

There are many homeless people and some day I wish to help those in need of help.
Marquisha Adams, Age 11, Boyd

My best piece of jewelry is my ring of friends.
Ann Robinson, Teacher, Wilder

Birds can't fly as high as my imagination.
Barbie Sherman, Age 12, Pittman

Playing on a losing team with friends is better than playing on a winning team with enemies.
Adam Brown, Age 11, Phelps

Never play in a poison ivy patch.
Jason Elliott, Age 10, Twain

Drinking water from the far side of the glass does not help hiccups, it just gets water all over you.
Nikki Smith, Age 14, Jarrett

You can't always win at tether ball.
Ryan Patrick Murphy, Age 11, Rountree

People can all do different things.
Andrea Orr, Age 9, Gray

WHAT I'VE LEARNED SO FAR IS . . .

If you don't study and your dog does, you will get a smart dog and a dumb boy.
Jimmy Thach, Age 10, Cowden

After teaching 26 years, quiet is strong; loud is weak.
Chuck Ramsey, Teacher, Parkview

To love.
Courtney Patrick, Age 6, Portland

Friends aren't always friends.
Thanh Duc Nguyin, Age 17, Central

How to read – It helps me know what those words under the pictures mean.
Sara Holt, Age 5, Sherwood

It is necessary to feel needed.
Jennifer Crouch, Age 15, Kickapoo

Never bowl in your socks.
Jamie Sparks, Age 12, Pittman

When your day slips out of gear, there is nothing wrong with letting it roll in neutral.
Matt Hufft, Age 16, Glendale

I do not like my sister doing cheers because she does not make sense.
Abigail Noelle Ragain, Age 8, Truman

WHAT I'VE LEARNED SO FAR IS . . .

If you ask your grandparents for money for no good reason, they will give it to you.
Jared Huddleston, Age 12, Pittman

It's not smart to talk back to a teacher.
Cryssi Buchanan, Age 11, Jeffries

Lizards don't sweat.
Jonathan Bailey, Age 7, Gray

My students have taught me more than any book could.
Nancy Goldsberry, Teacher, Robberson

No matter how many times I ask my mother or my father after they say no, it's still the same answer.
Greg Sullivan, Age 10, Cowden

Some grownups never act grown up even when they're old.
Jennifer Pearson, Age 13, Jarrett

Teaching elementary art requires a high energy level – and you must be very fast at the paper cutter.
Judy Wells, Teacher, Twain

The week is better when it ends on Wednesday.
Jamayla Coursey, Age 13, Reed

When you get your pictures back you show them off by saying they're terrible.
Brooke Barefield, Age 8, Truman

WHAT I'VE LEARNED SO FAR IS . . .

➤ Trying to get someone you love to stop smoking is hard.
Jennifer Flett, Age 10, Pittman

✂ Red fingernail polish is hard to put on by yourself.
Kahley Fiala, Age 6, Wilder

➤ It is important for me to learn how to read because if I did not know how to read I could be dead now because you have to read signs.
Chandra Cowens, Age 11, Boyd

✂ Never tear a paper up if you don't know what it is.
Amanda Woods, Age 9, Twain

➤ No matter how long the weekend is, it is never long enough.
Tracy Snodgrass, Teacher, Campbell

✂ No one will ever be as happy for me as I am for myself.
Emily Bell, Age 15, Kickapoo

➤ Your family is there for you when you want them to be and when you don't.
Laurel Edwards, Age 12, Jarrett

✂ You can look at everything in more than one way.
Nicholas Spradlin, Age 4, McDaniel
Early Childhood Program

➤ School is an interruption in life.
Teresa Mui, Age 11, Gray

WHAT I'VE LEARNED SO FAR IS . . .

If you are making a C in art, life goes on.
Wes Davis, Age 13, Reed

WHAT I'VE LEARNED SO FAR IS . . .

➡ That a doohickey can be anything.
Shaun Thompson, Age 10, Jeffries

✂ *No one* cooks better than Grandma.
Brian Ford, Age 17, Kickapoo

➡ My brother always says the grade I'm in is a sissy grade, after he already passed it.
Angela Becraft, Age 11, Mann

✂ I can share with people I don't like.
Tanya Davis, Age 9, Bingham

➡ I'm going to die someday, so I'll live the best life I possibly can – I'll have to try to enjoy school . . .
Louis Balsamo, Age 14, Jarrett

✂ Just because you're not the winner, doesn't mean you're the loser.
James Hyden, Age 10, Pittman

➡ Five girls can overpower one boy.
Josh Goodwin, Age 8, Truman

✂ If somebody throws up it sort of smells a little bit gross.
Joy Percifield, Age 7, Weaver

➡ There is only one person who knows what the future holds and keeps all His promises.
Tony Weatherford, Age 11, Twain

WHAT I'VE LEARNED SO FAR IS . . .

My mom has so many children she thinks she's rich.
Harry Willis, Age 6, Wilder

If you tell one friend a secret, he tells the other friend.
Jeremy McCandless, Age 10, Pittman

Things you spill will stain.
Michael Hampton, Age 8, Gray

Nobody can solve your problems for you.
Adelia Ward, Age 16, Central

Not to be afraid of death, because it's going to come sooner or later.
Hillary Van Hook, Age 12, Mann

The environment needs me, and there are millions of things I can do to help it.
Nicole Leaver, Age 9, Bingham

Never give a baby food and stand in front of him.
Emily Morrison, Age 11, Disney

Swimming against the current will make you a stronger person.
Darleen Anderson, Parent Educator
Parents As Teachers

Teenagers with boyfriends live on the phone.
Heather Means, Age 10, Jeffries

WHAT I'VE LEARNED SO FAR IS . . .

Don't wake up your parents.
> *Crystal Tracy, Age 10, Portland*

Life is more funner than anything.
> *Joah Beagley, Age 9, Gray*

To be a little bit more self–sacrificing.
> *Brett Macomber, Age 12, Field*

It is a long way to Chicago in a car.
> *Josh Wilkinson, Age 11, Twain*

When thinking up trouble, just think it and don't do it.
> *Steve Austin, Age 13, Pleasant View Middle*

That I am a democrat.
> *Kelly Goodman, Age 9, Bingham*

54 women working together under one roof make life interesting.
> *Terieca Branson, Secretary, McDaniel*

Teachers know when you're not in the bathroom.
> *Carrie Porter, Age 14, Kickapoo*

If I gave a nickel to my sister every time she told on me and a quarter to my brother every time he got in trouble, they'd be rich.
> *Brandie Ziegelbein, Age 11, Jeffries*

WHAT I'VE LEARNED SO FAR IS . . .

Grandparents are special.
Matthew Looker, Age 7, Gray

There is a very fine line between fishing and standing on the shore looking like an idiot.
Brad Vaughan, Age 17, Parkview

Not to pick on someone because he is different.
Austin Butts, Age 10, Study

How to bowl – it's OK to get gutter balls.
Wendy Felton, Age 5, Sherwood

My children are my greatest accomplishment so far.
Donna Prince, Secretary, Boyd

You're going to use everything you know sooner or later.
Heather Conn, Age 12, Weller

If you color hard your crayon will be gone.
Nate Marks, Age 9, Bingham

When one child is on a teeter totter and asks, "Why won't this go?" don't laugh, but explain how to make it go."
Leslie Strange Robinson, Teacher, Portland

It's never too early to study.
Josh Kirkpatrick, Age 11, Gray

WHAT I'VE LEARNED SO FAR IS . . .

Illustrated by Shiloh Peters, Age 9, Fremont

When you try to sneak out of the house when your mom's facing the other way, she will say, "Come back here right now!"
Jana Marie Stevens, Age 8, Mann

WHAT I'VE LEARNED SO FAR IS . . .

It isn't easy being new.
Michelle Griffin, Age 10, Field

The people on Madison Avenue run our lives.
Danny Ericsson, Age 15, Central

Red is special.
Kim Loftis, Age 6, Portland

D.A.R.E. is cool.
D. J. Nunn, Age 11, Twain

Being different is not as bad as some people think – I'm left–handed and a girl and I turned out fine.
Kristi German, Age 12, Pleasant View Middle

Not everybody cares about our Earth, and not everybody cares about other people.
Rick Novak, Age 9, Bingham

The harder I think, the more I can't.
Rebecca Drury, Age 12, Pershing

Yams are not made to eat – I should feed them to the dog.
Daniel Bordner, Age 8, Rountree

If you don't have any money, shopping isn't very fun.
Stacy Markham, Age 10, Mann

WHAT I'VE LEARNED SO FAR IS . . .

All sorts of kids have different ideas about what good behavior is.

John Durden, Bus Driver

You can't fool with parents to get out of things like why the cookies are all gone, or how come you are not going to eat your peas.

Zachary Kovarik Stevens, Age 8, Mann

Christmas trees are just pine trees any other time of year.

Joanna Sturhahn, Age 16, Kickapoo

Life is short. If you don't stop and enjoy it, you might just miss it.

Matthew Graham, Age 10, Field

Just because someone has a brand-new cherry red Porsche doesn't mean they are better than you, but it's nice to know them.

April Hill, Age 16, Central

I'm glad to be in America.

Brady Fast, Age 7, Gray

If you smile when you feel grouchy, no one will know except your husband.

Aldine Hilton, Teacher, Delaware

To trust my mom and dad.

Clint Bartley, Age 11, Pepperdine

To never stick your finger in an electrical socket.

Brandon Eckelmann, Age 9, Bingham

WHAT I'VE LEARNED SO FAR IS . . .

Life is great and I can be whatever I want.
Doug Wrinkle, Custodian, Portland

No one is perfect, no one is supposed to be perfect.
Dana Logsdon, Age 12, Pleasant View Middle

How the body works.
Logan Nothause, Age 6, Twain

The higher the grade, the more you have to think.
Natanael Herman, Age 11, Boyd

Little children always give you their honest opinion on the way you look; especially when you don't want to hear it.
Jennifer Eaton, Age 17, Kickapoo

You should always do what you think is right and not what your friends think is right.
Andrew Schillinger, Age 10, Gray

If you make a mistake, it doesn't mean you're stupid.
Rachel Lauren Parker, Age 8, Mann

Life is like a video game and you only have one quarter – give it your best.
Joe DeVries, Age 12, Pershing

Your life is getting shorter while your mind is getting bigger.
John Anno, Age 11, Jeffries

WHAT I'VE LEARNED SO FAR IS . . .

The winner of a fight is the one who stops it.
Chris Tabor, Age 10, Pleasant View

A flower must go through a lot of dirt before it blooms.
Sandy Rhodes, Teacher, McGregor

If there is a feather in your chicken, don't eat it.
John Waterman, Age 14, Reed

Check and make sure or guess and pay the price.
Taylor Stevenson, Age 10, Field

Don't just give around the holidays, give around all the days.
Sheri Stouder, Age 12, Jarrett

To act responsibly and act like a young lady and to act just like I was thirty years old.
Kathryn Whitney, Age 8, Field

Life has just about as much fizz as the person shaking the bottle.
Jane Green, Librarian, Doling

You may be born in a horse stall, but that doesn't make you a horse.
Jennifer Valentine, Age 11, Twain

Population rates of our state and others are going up and if we're not careful, we'll become extinct along with animals and forests.
Emily Compton, Age 10, Sunshine

WHAT I'VE LEARNED SO FAR IS . . .

Illustrated by Geoff Stufflebam, Age 10, Wilder

You don't go to bed with gum in your mouth
because in the morning it's in your hair.
Angela Telscher, Age 9, Delaware

WHAT I'VE LEARNED SO FAR IS . . .

✏️ To be quiet in school.
>> *Jennifer Eddings, Age 7, Williams*

✂️ When making bread with a class of second graders, make sure all finger bandages are removed *before* kneading the dough!
>> *Janice Hampton, Teacher/Librarian*
>> *Portland/McGregor*

✏️ If you don't pay attention in class, when the teacher calls on you, you're likely to say, "Huh?"
>> *Heidi Wunderlich, Age 11, Gray*

✂️ Not to sneak out when you have a dog.
>> *Cameron McCarter, Age 14, Cherokee*

✏️ Sometimes boys can be nice, but I tell you they can sometimes be as mean as a pig that just lost its ears.
>> *Lauren Gruchala, Age 7, Field*

✂️ It's easier to love a girl from another state than one that lives around the corner from you.
>> *Clayton Fewell, Age 18, Central*

✏️ Never leave the garbage can lids off or white worms will come.
>> *Thomas Wilder, Age 8, Mann*

✂️ If you loan someone something, you should take collateral.
>> *Ryan Anderson, Age 11, Gray*

✏️ The dentist knows when you haven't brushed your teeth.
>> *Brandon Lee Sweet, Age 13, Field*

WHAT I'VE LEARNED SO FAR IS . . .

For every 24 hour day, you have 25 hours of work.
Steven Nimmo, Age 15, Glendale

There are a lot of questions out in the world.
Jennifer Jones, Age 12, Rountree

Teachers the older kids say are so mean can be very nice and very sweet.
Amber Lee Cuff, Age 11, Pershing

If you hate math, you had better be somewhere else besides the classroom.
Ashley Peebles, Age 8, Field

Guys are just like little boys, they always want to "play" first.
April Dibber, Age 16, Central

My mom taught me how to do music.
Dustin McKenney, Age 6, Watkins

If mom says no, you should ask grandma.
Karen Dann, Age 10, Twain

Life is a bore until you fix it.
Tom Nourse, Age 11, Field

Kindergartners like to listen to third graders read.
Kate Underwood, Age 8, Gray

WHAT I'VE LEARNED SO FAR IS . . .

TV and candy are better than homework.
Larissa Hamelton, Age 12, Cowden

If someone doesn't have a crayon, you share.
Joshua Wright, Age 7, Boyd

Patience *is* an attainable skill.
Claire Cobb, Teacher, Twain

Nintendo games leave you broke!
Luke Burney, Age 12, Pleasant View Middle

To be nice to people and not hit people not in any way and to be good to people and I'll try to be nicer to people and not hit them.
Grant Sparks, Age 8, Field

If you call people names it doesn't feel so good to them and after a while your conscience starts bothering you.
Andrea Graves, Age 11, York

Goldfish can't live in the water out of the faucet.
Dong Suh, Age 11, Gray

When you try to sneak out of the house when your mom's facing the other way, she will say, "Come right back here, now!"
Jana Marie Stevens, Age 8, Mann

Moms can read your mind.
Lacy Mayes, Age 10, Study

WHAT I'VE LEARNED SO FAR IS . . .

No one can change a man but a man.
Melissa Cavins, Age 16, Central

Not to play football with people double my weight.
Jimmy Ashley, Age 11, Twain

Friendship is just as important as knowledge.
Bradlee Monson, Age 10, Field

I have the best job in the world and occasionally I hate the best job in the world.
Pat Horn, Counselor, Portland

Intolerance is worse than ignorance.
Jeni Shapiro, Age 17, Kickapoo

Everyone has a very special talent and you should not make fun of the person who is different.
SuLynn Greene, Age 12, Jarrett

To never stick my finger in my turtle's shell.
Ricky Stennett, Age 10, Westport

How to turn a cartwheel and make my hair touch the ground.
Meagan McCullough, Age 5, Sherwood

A listening ear reflects a caring heart.
Georgia Turner, Secretary, Sunshine

WHAT I'VE LEARNED SO FAR IS . . .

Never give a baby food and stand in front of him.
Emily Morrison, Age 11, Disney

WHAT I'VE LEARNED SO FAR IS . . .

The bigger you are is not always the harder you fall.
Wes McNew, Age 14, Study

Words, numbers, how to spell things, and that's all.
Wade Buchanan, Age 6, Twain

When you ride your bike fast you always get a bug in your eye.
Maggie Stafford, Age 10, Mann

Friends and fights don't mix.
Sara Smith, Age 11, Jeffries

Do not try to kiss a girl or she will smack you.
Curtis Montgomery, Age 8, Pepperdine

Hopefully a lot less than what I'm going to learn.
Kyle Gorden, Age 15, Glendale

Having a 30 minute time limit on the phone is no fun.
Rhonda Self, Age 12, Bowerman

Reading is a lot funner than just sitting.
Katie Burrows, Age 8, Sequiota

Sixth grade doesn't just mean that you're the oldest of the school – it means responsibility.
Misty Finley, Age 11, Boyd

WHAT I'VE LEARNED SO FAR IS . . .

The best teachers aren't always the nicest.
Chris Tabor, Age 10, Pleasant View

How to sweet–talk the copying machine and keep the coffee hot until school is over.
Darlene Rubenstein, Resource Aide, Bingham

You're always too young to die.
Laurie Weiss, Age 12, Pershing

Persistence is not always good.
Thanh Duc Nguyen, Age 17, Central

Peter Pan helps people fly so that they won't be afraid of heights.
Matt Schutten, Age 7, Williams

How to find sunshine in clouds.
Pat Renner, Teacher, Portland

If you throw your pillow at a cat, you won't feel any better.
Grant Oglesby, Age 11, Disney

In the great scheme of things, my students are the chocolate chip cookies and paperwork, bus duty and indoor recesses are the sour lemon balls.
Sherri Adams, Teacher, Bingham

How to spell a lot of hard words and how to put on a good play.
Aaron Michael Collins, Age 9, Twain

WHAT I'VE LEARNED SO FAR IS . . .

✏️ When it's time for recess all that's left is jump ropes, which is girly stuff.
> *Brad Thuro, Age 9, Gray*

✂️ To not scream in stores.
> *Jennifer Hunt, Age 6, Cowden*

✏️ When it comes to love, guys aren't as tough as they seem.
> *Enoch Ennis, Age 14, Study*

✂️ If you say you can, you can. If you say you can't, you can't.
> *Sarah Naasz, Age 11, Mann*

✏️ Brothers are worse than they look.
> *Emily Blincow, Age 8, Sequiota*

✂️ Friends are the best medicine for loneliness.
> *Emily Bingham, Age 12, Pittman*

✏️ Be careful in how you choose your words– not communicating effectively can be the downfall of any organization.
> *Gary Eisley, Head Custodian, Bingham*

✂️ Not to forget a true friend for a more popular person.
> *Reyanna Buchholz, Age 10, Jeffries*

✏️ To run and hide when my mom tells me to practice violin.
> *Ashley Peebles, Age 8, Field*

WHAT I'VE LEARNED SO FAR IS . . .

If you buy a vehicle and you have a lot of friends without vehicles, you should charge them gas money or you could become poor real quick.
Tim Williams, Age 16, Central

People who say they're your friends, then use you, are really not your friends.
Ryan Zimmerman, Age 11, Mann

You can't fake wisdom.
Meredith Ashworth, Teacher, Boyd

Growing up takes 13 years, then you're a teenager!
Sarah Spallinger, Age 8, Campbell

Never go to McDonald's when you feel sick.
Daniela Novotny, Age 10, Twain

You're never too old to make bubble beards when you're in the bathtub.
Sarra Casler, Age 17, Kickapoo

When I feel bad I talk to my mom or dad and then I feel better.
Shaun Munday, Age 7, Boyd

When you get a pool, you get a lot of new friends.
Beth Breite, Age 11, Gray

Not to wait till Sunday to go to the library.
Nicholas Kasparek, Age 10, Pershing

WHAT I'VE LEARNED SO FAR IS . . .

You can't touch a star.
Dustin Burns, Age 7, York

Illustrated by David Maissner, Age 12, Mann

WHAT I'VE LEARNED SO FAR IS . . .

➤ Teachers aren't so easy to bribe as parents.
Reed Hopper, Age 12, Jeffries

✂ I have to wear glasses even if I don't want to so I won't be blind.
Mark Baker, Age 9, York

➤ If you mess with girls, they will kick you.
Bobby Spurgeon, Age 12, Campbell

✂ I don't have to do anything that anyone wants me to do.
Leann Daniels, Age 11, Twain

➤ I'm not stupid, I was just never told.
Janet Chambers, Age 17, Kickapoo

✂ Raising kids is not for cowards.
Vicky Turner, Library Aide, Boyd

➤ God will always love you, even though you sin.
Carrie Cathren Siegmann, Age 8, Mann

✂ When you're in kindergarten, enjoy the naps while you get them.
Sara Reubell, Age 11, Disney

➤ Being the middle child isn't always easy.
Alexa Keehn, Age 10, Sequiota

WHAT I'VE LEARNED SO FAR IS . . .

When I go under water not to open my mouth.
Lee Ruff, Age 7, Twain

When the teacher says quiet, you then best get quiet.
Erin Reeves, Age 10, Study

Good judgement comes from experience, but experience comes from bad judgement.
Michelle Orndorff, Teacher, Delaware

Some people have dreams and some don't.
Dinsel Coble, Age 12, Robberson

The strongest hearts are also the most fragile.
Jamie Trant, Age 16, Central

You can't stop a presidential candidate from arguing.
Elizabeth, Age 11, Jeffries

If you leave laundry in a room by itself it will multiply.
Toni Palmer, Teacher, Gray

When you're in a hurry, the rest of the world isn't.
Jody Burrow, Age 18, Kickapoo

Girls can do things boys can't.
Becky Snead, Age 9, Pershing

WHAT I'VE LEARNED SO FAR IS . . .

➤ I haven't learned anything.
Scott Dickerson, Age 6, Twain

✂ I can't play with my sister at recess because my sister needs to meet other people.
Anonymous, Age 8, Pershing

➤ If you try to "go with" two girls, you soon won't have any girls.
Eddy Bauer, Age 12, Cherokee

✂ Don't ride your bike with your shoes untied.
Rachal Hallman, Age 9, Williams

➤ Give a child everything he needs and half of what he asks for.
Jan Woodland, Teacher, Mann

✂ Being powerless against some form of social force is not a justification for apathy.
Joan Liu, Age 16, Kickapoo

➤ To want what's worth wanting.
Robin Letterman, Age 11, Boyd

✂ Don't make an issue out of something unless it will make a difference 10 years from now.
Carolyn Hall, Teacher, Bingham

➤ To wish either vegetables tasted like ice cream or parents didn't make you eat them.
Kendall Eberlin, Age 10, Sequiota

WHAT I'VE LEARNED SO FAR IS . . .

➡ You'd better play hard when you're young because you are older longer than you are young.
Miranda Kathleen Smith, Age 11, Cowden

✂ Never take a test without reading it.
Nichole Powell, Age 9, Twain

➡ Dissecting grasshoppers and worms isn't that bad, but I haven't tried frogs yet.
Erin Quinn, Age 12, Cherokee

✂ What candy does when you eat too much of it.
Justin K. Hurbrader, Age 11, Jeffries

➡ If you jump off the Empire State building you will usually die.
Jorden Michael Hyde, Age 8, Mann

✂ You must pick up trash, because it makes the world cleaner, and I like clean.
Alicia Moore, Age 5, Sherwood

➡ Fathers always give in quicker than mothers.
Amy Rockafellow, Age 12, Pershing

✂ Your heart beats over 1,000 times a day.
Tim Casteel, Age 10, Bissett

➡ The best subject man can study is himself.
Jeff Carl, Age 17, Kickapoo

WHAT I'VE LEARNED SO FAR IS . . .

illustrated by Tommy Gibson, Age 11, Wilder

You don't bother a snake or you might even get wrapped up by a python and you can't breathe and it kills you and eats you for dinner and it will hurt and you will be poisoned and you will have to go to the doctor.

Ronnie Higgins
Age 7, Weaver

WHAT I'VE LEARNED SO FAR IS . . .

Leaving my best friend was the worst thing I ever had to do.
Constance Forsythe, Age 12, Study

Not to eat an onion–coated chili dog while on a date.
Jamie Ulrich, Age 16, Kickapoo

Air Jordans don't make you jump any higher.
Adam Perryman, Age 11, Jeffries

To color in the lines and spell NO!
Lindsey Garcia, Age 6, Twain

Teachers aren't perfect – they also make mistakes.
Ian Hendry, Age 10, Sherwood

To do the two–step with my dog.
Kira Lowrey, Age 8, Bissett

No matter how old you are, you are still your parents' baby.
Jaren Appleton, Age 11, Bingham

Never to make fun of someone else.
Shawna Ruth Warren, Age 9, Mann

Life is hard and sometimes fun but with diseases going around, you have to be tough.
Swraj Arora, Age 10, Twain

WHAT I'VE LEARNED SO FAR IS . . .

TV spoils your brain.
Portland Lloyd, Age 6, Cowden

Instead of filling out the race questions on applications, I would rather just check a box that says "human being."
Joan Liu, Age 16, Kickapoo

Climbing on a shed causes trouble if you fall through.
Wesley Henline, Age 9, York

Students say, "My mother taught me how to read."
Betty Maples, Teacher, Twain

A teacher can also be a friend.
Joy Williams, Age 11, Twain

When we're assigned too much, even good things get lost in the shuffle.
Peggy Morrow, Teacher, Twain

The length of your day depends on your last hour of class.
Luke Forschler, Age 15, Glendale

The posters hung the highest are always the ones to fall down.
Jane Adamson, Teacher, Twain

Everybody is different and life can be surprising and exciting.
Gary McDowell, Age 12, Weller

WHAT I'VE LEARNED SO FAR IS . . .

If a cat scratches me, I don't hold it anymore.
Lindsay Wakeem, Age 5, Sherwood

It's not easy to be the person your mom and dad want you to be.
Anonymous, Age 12, Study

How to share my feelings with others.
Ryda Nguyen, Age 11, Twain

Everyone has a right.
Tasha Stafford, Age 6, Twain

Life's not a piece of cake – I like pie better anyway.
Chris Watts, Age 12, Jeffries

Math is not so hard when you use your fingers.
Johnny Merrifield, Age 8, Twain

You have to work hard if you want to get anywhere in life, especially if you have a girlfriend.
Jeremy Cook, Age 11, Mann

Nothing is impossible for God.
Jon Kelley, Age 8, Twain

Your imagination can take you farther than any other form of transportation.
Carissa Carey, Age 15, Central

WHAT I'VE LEARNED SO FAR IS . . .

To stay away from dogs named "Bear"!
Josh Roberts, Age 12, Pershing

About pirates, and Indians, and Pilgrims, spiders, and alligators, and snakes.
Rachael Salveter, Age 9, Bingham

You can never ask for anything better than a good mystery novel and a warm blanket on a stormy day.
Erica Hertzog, Age 11, Field

"When I was your age" stories are never true.
Mike Marchand, Age 12, Phelps

Expectation should be more of ourselves and maybe not so much of others.
Ken Henry, Custodian, Westport

How to borrow, and I'm good at it too.
Chris Hill, Age 8, Sherwood

Believe your teacher when she says you'll use your Algebra again—you will . . . in Geometry, Algebra Two, Calculus, etc.
Ami Slavin, Age 16, Glendale

The people who complain the most are usually part of the problem.
Christy Carlson, Age 17, Kickapoo

To sit by a boy and not fight.
Heather Blum, Age 8, Bissett